POAC
PIE

ALSO AVAILABLE FROM ALAN SUTTON

The Village Doctor
When Village Bells Were Silent
by Fred Archer

ENGLISH COUNTRY TALES

POACHER'S PIE

Fred Archer

ALAN SUTTON
1987

ALAN SUTTON PUBLISHING
BRUNSWICK ROAD · GLOUCESTER

First published 1976
by Hodder and Stoughton Limited

This paperback edition published 1987

British Library Cataloguing in Publication Data

Archer, Fred, *1915–*
Poacher's pie.
1. Ashton under Hill (Hereford and Worcester)—Social life and customs
I. Title
942.4′49 DA690.A815

ISBN 0-86299-428-4

Cover photograph by Martin Latham

Printed in Great Britain by
The Guernsey Press Company Limited
Guernsey, Channel Islands

AUTHOR'S NOTE

It is debatable whether pure history exists. It does rather depend whether it is written by an Englishman, a Frenchman or a German. Bias is inevitable and inbuilt. I never set out to make this book historically precise, though it does take in various historical events and the dates of wars and floods, royal weddings and coronations are correct to the best of my knowledge.

I have put some people in this book by their real names—the Boswell brothers and Lovely Hill, for instance, who were tried for murder at Worcester Assizes in 1890, and Fred Stephens, the man they were accused of killing. Keeper Wasley appears under his own name too, along with Charles Cook, Barlow Cole, and my Uncle Fred, and of course the Duc d'Aumale and his nephew the Duc d'Orleans who lived at Wood Norton Hall during the period and entertained the crowned and deposed heads of Europe to hunting and shooting. However, the Bradfields, the Garrets, the Bostocks, the Fosters are composite characters with invented names to cover the amalgamation of some typical men and women of the Vale of Evesham, or Asum, as we call it, who lived on the black soil a lifetime ago.

I knew Lovely Hill as an old man. I met him sometimes in the fruit market with my father. I also met Fred Stephens' widow while I was at school. Mrs Stephens was a friend of my mother and I grew up listening to the talk of Wood Norton from Shepherd Tidmarsh who worked for Mr Randall. I was fortunate in being able to draw on the memories of a man who lived in the keeper's cottage next door to Fred Stephens, and Alfred Baker of Hipton Hill has also been a good first-hand source of information, as has Harvey Hunt and Jack Cook, late of Pinvin, whose talk is still flavoured by the cart horse age.

I should also like to thank the Editor of the *Evesham Journal*, C. W. Clarke, for the use of his files and for photographs, and Benjamin Cox, Chairman of the Vale of Evesham Historical Society, for kindly lending me some photographs of Wood Norton which appeared in his booklet *Wood Norton*, a valuable source of historical reference.

Fred Archer, 1976

CONTENTS

		page
1	At Carrants View	9
2	Domestic Service	17
3	Walking the Night	25
4	The Whistling Ploughman	31
5	The Royal Currant Jelly Boys	37
6	On the Black Soil	45
7	Asum's New Army	53
8	Trouble in the Woods	61
9	The Murder of Fred Stephens	67
10	The Search for Lovely Hill	73
11	Worcester Assizes	79
12	No Reprieve	87
13	The Executions	93
14	New Dukes for Old	99
15	A Right Royal Riot	107
16	Golden Gates, Tin Tabernacle	115
17	The Little Master of Men	123
18	Wooden Plough and Timber	135
19	A Day at the Seaside	145
20	The End of Utopia	157

ILLUSTRATIONS

facing page

Plum picking in the Vale 48

Among the strawberry rows 49

A pea-picking party rests its backs 49

The Duc d'Aumale[1] 64

The Duc d'Orleans[1] 64

The Golden Gates at Wood Norton[2] 65

Asum waits to greet the guests for the royal wedding[2] 96

The tin tabernacle in Asum[3] 96

The Duc d'Orleans with his sister and some guests at a shoot[2] 97

The bag at the end of the royal shoot[2] 97

The author's father and mother 112

Uncle Fred 112

A tabber and tut band[4] 113

The Pinvin Sports Committee, 1912[4] 113

Key to acknowledgments

[1] Victoria and Albert Museum

[2] Benjamin Cox

[3] The *Evesham Journal*

[4] *Warwickshire and Worcestershire Life*

I

AT CARRANTS VIEW

I

At Carrants View

It's been said and rightly so that the Englishman's home is his castle. What were these castles in our village in the eighteen eighties? They are so near to me, so dear to me, the thoughts of Ashton in those not so distant days.

I picture Jack Bradfield's thatched cot, where the stair door faced the front door and the ripples of Bredon Hill paving stone formed a floor like a choppy sea as they lay, uneven as a ploughed field, leading to the black-leaded grate.

Here Bessie Bradfield sat with her five children home from school, while Milly the baby played on the rag rug.

The kettle boiled on the pot hooks, the saucepans simmered

lifting their black iron lids. One on each hob they stood. The large one held a rabbit with onions, turnips and dumplings. The smaller one boiled the potatoes. Five children sat around the American cloth covered table, each eating their piece—a crust of bread with plum jam. Jack had just returned for his evening meal.

He had been hedge cutting all day. This and catching rabbits was his winter's work in the field. A tall lean man, stooping early at forty, he arrived home carrying a log for the fire.

At six the stew was done and Jack sat in the wooden armchair at the head of the table, while Bessie ladled the liquor, the meat and the vegetables on to seven plates, plates that once were white, now spider-webbed with brown lines, patterns made by their journeying in and out of the black-leaded oven.

"Can I have his head, Mum?" the eldest boy, Reg, called from his place.

"Go on, boy," Jack said tiredly, while Reg cracked the rabbit's skull and ate the brains.

After the bread pudding sprinkled with a few currants, Jack wiped his mouth saying, "A nice bit a fittle, Mother."

The tea was stewed as always, black from the crock pot off the hob, while Bessie poured the skim milk from Stallard's, who made butter for the better off, with a little sugar into each of the cups.

The evening meal was over.

The accommodation of Carrants View consisted of the house place, as it was known, a pantry, and the wash house with an earthern floor, a brown crock sink and two buckets. One of these was full of water from the well, the other to take the left overs, if ever there were left overs from the table, and the potato peelings and turnip tops for the pig wash tub outside.

The stairs were steep and rickety, leading straight into a landing bedroom. Here Reg and Ron slept on an iron bedstead with tarnished brass knobs at the bed ends.

A rough hewn elm door with heavy iron hinges and a wooden latch, black as the tarred beams overhead, led into Jack and Bessie's room. The ceiling was pitched as the pitch of the thatched roof, leaving only a five foot width of flat plastered ceiling, whitewashed as near white as lime and water brushed on to the lath and plaster would allow. Layer upon layer of wallpaper had covered the sloping walls and the purlin beam. Bessie's last effort at papering was a pattern of roses and violets.

The brazen bedstead stood where it only could stand, under the five-foot-wide ceiling, where Jack could stand up straight at the foot of the bed to hang his working clothes on the wicker-seated chair. Bessie kept her few clothes in an old red mahogany-looking chest of drawers under the beam and in a brown, half-rusty metal chest.

On Bessie's side of the bed Philip, the five-year-old, still slept cramped in his cot, bought at the rummage sale when he was a baby. Milly lay cosy in her orange box, while through the door in a small box room type dormitory, lit only by a glass pane in the thatch, Doris and Kate shared a bed.

"Peaceful in our little cabin, Missus," Jack said, as he wound up the grandfather clock. This proud possession stood between the sideboard and little harmonium.

"Yes," Bessie smiled, as she put the cat out to get his living round the nearby barn where the rats and mice were nibbling corn. While the village slept Tiddles helped to keep the vermin down.

The children woke as Jack and Bessie creaked up the stairs. They turned over under the blankets, listening for a moment to the squeak of mice in the straw thatch and the occasional rustle of the sparrows spending the night under the eaves.

Two sighs as the Bradfields sank into the breast feathers of many Christmas cockerels in the bed tick, one puff and the candle was out. Weary bones were resting.

"One day more, one day less," Jack whispered to his wife.

"You shouldn't, our Jack, tempt the one above," Bessie answered. "We be in his hands."

Jack thought of his seven children and his wife struggling on ten shillings a week. Then the family slept, sheltered by strong beams, wattle and daub walls and a straw roof. They knew no other life. Jack and Bessie had lived fifteen years together at

Carrants View. Their possessions were so few, yet their reasonably good health and a simple ignorance of the wealth amassed by the few, was a stay which could not be shaken by any man's idle words.

Their routine was so much akin to the birds' and beasts' around them. They knew no other, they apparently wished it to be no different. When the wind howled down the oversize chimney the cottage represented to them a refuge from bitter weather at night, weather which Jack had to endure every day, while Bessie clad and shod her children for school.

In the morning Jack primed the water pump and with a few strokes on the handle he filled his galvanized bucket with pure water from an underground spring thirty feet below the garden. The dry sticks flared in the grate, the kettle sang, Bessie made the tea, cut the loaf and fried a little fat bacon in a frying pan with a round handle which hung from the pot hooks.

Putting his arm on her shoulder Jack said, "Never mind the bacon, 'tis a bit reasty now. But come Christmas we ull have our pig killed. Then we can live a bit better."

Out in the sty the Bradfields' pig looked over the door for his breakfast.

While still chewing his bread and bacon, Jack dipped a bowl into the hogshead barrel and poured a mixture of swill into the pig bucket. A handful of meal gave the swill a bit more substance and greedily and noisily the cottage pig sucked the food from the trough.

"Your bread and cheese is wrapped un your kerchief in your frail basket and I've put you a bottle of tea for your midday."

"Oi thank ya, Bessie. That ull kip me going and the gaffer ull bring me a drop of cider, happen."

Next door Beattie Bradfield lived alone, a widow on the half crown a week parish relief. At seventy-two she still worked a full day in the fields picking and pulling, cutting and loading the farm and garden crops of the Vale. In the cold March gilly fields, tying the raffia around the blood-red flowers, her face glowed with a warmth which could almost be felt.

Beattie had lost her husband when he fell from a waggon-load of straw, the same year as poor George Baker got strangled with the chaff cutter in Mr Cambridge's barn. Mr Cambridge was a fair gaffer and always found the men work on wet days. Not like most farmers who sent them home and stopped their wages.

When it rained all farm men used Midland Railway wheat sacks as capes over their shoulders to keep out the wet. George had tied his in place in the usual country manner with a bit of farmer's glory, or binder twine, tied at the collar. A handy man was George. But this time he got caught up in the pulleys in the barn and the sack wound round the chaff cutter's shafting until he was strangled by the neck.

Beattie's son, Jack was good to her; so were the youngsters. Reg carried her bucket of water from their pump and Ron did her "harronds", fetching her bits of shopping and her supper beer.

The Bradfields' cottages were bare and inadequate by modern standards, but where the Boswell family were reared was what we would call battery housing today. Here at Beechwood Cottage a family of ten slept in one bedroom and a landing.

It's true two died of what was then known as consumption. One saw the rosy cheeks, the tell-tale glow which seemed a sign of health, suddenly turn to the haunted look of high cheek bones and sunken eyes, the hacking cough, and in their prime at twenty-one years of age they faded away and filled two more spaces in our churchyard. Two sons, Joe and Sam remained, growing into men with muscles of iron.

Caleb, the father of them all, worked now at hedging and ditching after suffering a strained heart and rupture through carrying a sack of wheat under each arm for a half a crown.

2

DOMESTIC SERVICE

2

Domestic Service

THE MEN ON THE LAND HAD MUCH TO COMPLAIN about in the late nineteenth century. Low wages, long hours sweating in the hayfield, winter time standing in water-flushed ditches in boots and gaiters before the Wellington boots appeared in the shops to keep their feet dry. But the men rarely came home at night from the fields with an empty frail basket. A thrifty man, because it was thrift, brought something home, something he looked upon as a gift of the gods of nature—a rabbit perhaps, a few windfall apples, a couple of swedes or some mushrooms.

But how the women had to scrape for a reasonable living! It seemed that they were tied to their jobs even more than the menfolk. Single women in domestic service took a gamble when they were hired to do the mistress's will for twelve months.

One who cleaned and cooked many years ago was Alice Croft who went into service at thirteen years of age with the Fosters at Umberlands Farm, a few miles from Ashton, or Ayshton, as we called it, almost swallowing the 't', so that it came out very like 'Asum', which was Evesham of course and quite a different matter. Alice never complained about the life in a farm house so many years ago. She was the younger of two servants who shared the attic bedroom. Her life was so busy she hardly had time to think how many hours she worked. At half past five every morning she and Nellie got up, lit the range and, if visitors were staying, they cooked breakfast, boiling the water for the upstairs washbasins in an iron pot over the fire. The jugs of water were placed outside the bedroom doors and the boots and shoes taken down to the kitchen and blacked and shined until they could see their faces in the leather. All Alice could say was that the food was wholesome, but two shillings a week wages didn't go far.

But how different a life to service in a town! Alice and Nellie had their little compensations when they drove the pony and float to the hayfields with a clothes basket full of bread fresh from the bake oven and cheese, also home-made, with their own butter and boiled bacon for the men in the hayfields. Alice's master and mistress were chapel "tea-totals", so they took no cider to the fields, but an urn of hot strong tea to quench the thirst of the sweating haymakers.

There was little time to stay and joke with the young lads on the farm as Mrs Foster would be calling from the yard gate as she fed the following flock of hens on the bare patch in the orchard under the apple trees.

"Come on, you girls. There's work to do in the kitchen, Biddy-Biddy-Biddy," she called the fowl, as her voice 'ticed the hesitant broody hens from their nests in the cattle mangers.

But Alice and Nellie respected their employers. "They be good living folk, Master and Missus Foster," Alice said, and Nellie agreed they were real Christians, pointing out, "Master Foster do take off that stinking smock when he have foddered the cattle in the yard and puts on a dacent jacket for prayers."

Prayers were at nine in the great hall, which Nellie always used to consider a convenient arrangement.

"That saved I the performance beside the bed. 'Cos why should we trouble the Almighty aguyn? Thur must be a smartish wave a asking for favours like a gwain up to he about that hour a night."

Young Reg Bradfield started working at the farm and the cider sop breakfasts he had been used to at his last place were allowed no more.

Alice said, "He had bread and skim milk, same as us and thee knowst the skim milk is as blue as any whitstun. He couldn't run to belly on that frightened water."

The skim milk came straight from the separator, as Reg turned the handle. The cream went into vats for butter making and when it was ripe Reg had to turn the butter churn.

"We girls," Alice told me, "made the butter into pats and put the Missus's stamp on each un. An after we had scrubbed the place an scalded the milking buckets Reg said he could yut his fittle off the floor." They used wood ash from the dog grate in the hall twice a week on the milking buckets to make them shine. And the buckets the calves had their food in had to be just as clean.

Sunday or the weekends stayed in Alice's memory until today.

The potatoes were peeled on Saturday night and the vegetables got ready for the oven. No washing up was allowed on Sunday. All the crocks were put in a bath of water after meals, except the knives and forks. In the morning the Fosters drove their cob and four-wheeled carriage to the village Baptist chapel, while Alice and Nellie cooked the dinner, dressed in their black dresses and white aprons.

One Sunday Alice put on another frock but was soon told not to ape the gentry.

"Those walks on Sunday afternoon to the church in the next village gave us a change," Nellie said, "but we were timed half and hour to get there an hour in church and half and hour back."

I wondered sometimes how the comparatively well to do could put on thirteen-year-old girls, asking them what the sermon was about over tea where the bread was thick and the butter just a scrape.

After tea Alice, Nellie, Reg and others who were living in, brought the hard chairs down out of the attic for an evening of Victorian piety. Mr Foster preached in the big hall as the servants and his children sat and listened. Mrs Foster played Sankey hymns on the harmonium.

It's true it was the farmer's wish that his servants should grow in the fear of God, remain in their proper stations in life, work hard, live plainly and be respectable. Possibly Mr Foster was also intent that they should be a credit to Umberlands Farm, both at work and in their private lives.

One wonders whether he saw his men, his servant girls and dairy maids as a symbol of the good crops he grew, his tidy hay and corn ricks, neatly thatched, his shorthorn herd of cows and the fact that his fat lambs always won first prize at the local market.

Alice described how she had to pay for the crocks she broke one Sunday as she carried a loaded tray from the kitchen to the dining room. "Took a long time, you know, out of two shillings per week."

Reg Bradfield after his days in the fields ploughing, drilling, hay making and reaping wandered around the rick yard at Umberlands Farm. Among the nettles where Mr Foster or his wife had not searched he often found where a hen had laid astray. Perhaps a nest of twelve eggs dropped by a stately old Wyandotte who chose a quiet place away from the cattle mangers and the yap of Foster's terrier dog.

Reg was a honest worker but the days of skimmed milk sop breakfast, fat bacon dinners, and bread and scrape for tea became monotonous. The dinner wasn't so bad but the thick bread and the suggestion of butter on it at six every evening didn't satisfy a hungry young man. Quietly Reg filled his cap with the eggs and hid them behind the corn bin in the stable.

He took three however to the kitchen. Calling Alice aside he asked her to boil them in the big iron kettle which hung on the pot hooks from the sway over the kitchen fire.

"One for you Alice and two for me, along with tomorrow's bait. Boil them hard, ull ya?" he said. "Then they ull help the morsel of cheese down when my horses rest on the 'adlun."

Alice smiled and her red cheeks looked even redder as she said, "Well I never. Fancy you thinking of that, boiling eggs in kettles so the missus won't know."

As he came in to prayers that night and Mr Foster read from the black Book as big as the stable door, Reg reckoned if he hadn't searched where the Wyandotte laid, the eggs would soon have been addled.

Alice stayed a couple of years more, making four years at the monthly payment of eight shillings wages, then gave notice.

"Where do you think I went?" she asked me.

"Oh a bigger place I reckon, perhaps a country mansion."

"No, a public," she said. "The Miller's Arms at Broughton. Now they were a nice couple, quite young. Mind you, it wasn't proper for a girl to be seen in the bar and I was but seventeen and never allowed in there. Every morning at five o'clock we opened the windows to get rid of the smell of twist and stale beer. Then I had to scrub the floor, clean the bar and the spittoons. And twice a week there was the whitening to do."

This whitening was an old practice where every joint in between the stone slabbed floor was marked with a bat of whitening. It made the pub look like a draught board when the railway men came in for their six o'clock in the morning beer. The pubs were open all day until ten o'clock at night, and Alice had to be out in the kitchen cooking breakfast at six a.m.

"The landlord put the crock tots under the tapped barrels and served the men. I never touched a spot myself," she added. "Just home-made wine which Mother made. Wine tis a mocker, Mr Foster used to read out of the Bible, and it can be."

Alice married Reg Bradfield some years after and they lived in one of a row of cottages near the farm where he worked. The village where Reg and Alice lived for so many years had an odd custom. The girls didn't wear drawers. A village girl went for an interview with a lady for a position as maid and the lady asked her grandmother if the girl wore drawers.

"Oh no, M'm," her Granny said.

The lady replied, "I am glad. I don't believe in girls wearing drawers. It gives them ideas above their station."

Once Alice fell ill, in fact she was taken to hospital.

Four and a half gallons of mature rhubarb wine lay untapped in a barrel in their back kitchen. Bill Laxton, who had recently married, lived next door. So every night Bill and Reg went to bed well-primed with rhubarb wine.

"Tis my birthday today," Bill told Reg as they made for the rickyard one morning at six o'clock. "How about a session tonight, Reg?"

The two men sat by the fireside chimney and sang until bedtime, when Bill pottered cautiously down the path to join his wife next door, and fumbled his way to bed. In the candlelight his wife looked up from her pillow and saw Bill hanging on to the brass bed post at the foot of the bed, saying with tears in his eyes and almost afraid to let go the posts, "We have finished the rhubarb, Missus, and I do wish there had been a spring in the bottom of Bradfield's barrel, a spring as never runs dry."

"Come in the yer aside me, ya silly drunken crater," she replied, and he flopped on the bed and slept.

"I heard about it," Alice said, "but mind, if I had been at home that job wouldn't have happened, because I should have rationed it out. Moderation is my motto."

A great character, Alice. From the hard grind at Fosters' she had acquired a certain dignity which money would never buy. A lady describes her well.

3

WALKING THE NIGHT

3

Walking the Night

IN GENESIS CHAPTER 25 WE READ, "AND ESAU WAS a cunning hunter, a man of the field and Jacob was a plain man, dwelling in tents. And Isaac loved Esau, because he did eat of his venison."

So, since time began or rather since primitive man, hunting has been an instinct. Not an instinct for pleasure, but for survival.

The eternal question is how did the families in my little corner of England survive on meagre wages and tea kettle broth? The answer has resounded in my ears since I was a boy.

They poached.

How dreadful, I can hear voices saying, stealing.

Since Miss Campbell wrote, "All good gifts around us are sent from heaven above", the countryman could hardly be expected not to take just a small share of these gifts. The large families who survived the agricultural depression after 1879 lived not on ten, twelve or fourteen shillings a week, but partly on these gifts.

Joe Boswell and Sam had poached the slopes of Bredon Hill since their old Dad, Caleb, had taught them how to use the long net to catch the rabbits, how to set the wire snare and the gate net to catch the hares.

Caleb had known the time when the Game Laws forbade the allotment holder to snare a rabbit on his own allotment, and it was rough justice if he were caught, even when the rabbits were feeding off his cabbage.

I think of these days and never wonder why the labourer kept his stew jar full of the fur and feather of the land. It was also against the law to shoot a pheasant or partridge on a Sunday. Were the Victorian rulers who insisted that this law was kept so pious, so righteous? This was probably hypocrisy at its peak.

No wonder the village labourer worked six days a week and with stealth used his muzzle loaded gun on Sunday.

Sam and Joe Boswell knew the rules. They lived in a cottage owned by a lady of the village. The family's rent was two shillings and a penny per week.

It's true Sam was sent to goal for poaching on several occasions, but it was worth the risk. Sam's sense of humour remained—he sent the Governor of Gloucester gaol a couple of hares every Christmas.

Sam and Joe, and Reg Bradfield were the sort of men the village policeman avoided on his rounds. Passionate men, my Uncle Fred said, men who combed the autumn stubble netting partridges.

In his day old Caleb Boswell had made wicker funnels and driven the young birds to a dead end in broad daylight, capturing a number at one fell swoop, or he caught his pheasants by night with a tin of smoking sulphur on a long pole, which put the sleeping bird into a deeper sleep until it fell from its lofty perch. Smoking was not successful on a large scale. Had it been so there would have been no need to use the noisy gun and give the alert to the keeper.

Sam and Joe, however, used no guns as they took the game from the woods north of Bredon. A few oats or tail corn sprinkled in the tracks of the birds is soon eaten up where the hand-reared birds are plentiful. Then the Boswell boys set their snares in the runs, nooses made from twenty-four horse hairs plaited together and placed, pegged down at intervals, in the ride between the trees. All gaps were cunningly blocked up with bushes or even a net to stop the bird's passage.

Reg walked the woods under the moon when the leafless oaks were littered with gaudy cock birds. Carrying a long bamboo cane with a noose or snare at the end he quietly looped his bird, fluttering to the leaf-covered ground. There were no end of ways of catching them. Let me quote A. G. Stuart Wortley on the pheasant:

> No; he has not the poetry of the partridge, nor the romance of the grouse. He is a fowl, a barn-door fowl! A tame, polygamous foreign bird that, like the Cochin-China or the Guinea, can be tended by an old woman or caught by a boy. Those who shoot him perform no feat; they are not sportsmen—only specimens of the decadent aristocracy or inflated plutocracy of England; the "battue" is a foreign horror, the shooter no longer an English gentleman, but a Parisian "gommeux".

No I wouldn't go all the way with Wortley, but do see an ocean of difference between what he calls the battue and the rough shoot, where wild birds are walked up. It's a strange world when birds are fed as tame as fowls to be driven over the guns by beaters on an October Saturday.

Sam, Joe and Reg were happier in the open fields when the wind blew strong in their faces on dark nights netting rabbits. Here gamekeepers were seldom around, for the three poachers had their scouts out. Caleb would be in the pub drinking with a keeper and watching the policeman's movements.

Surely the most humane way to control the over-population of rabbits was to catch them in the long net and kill them in a brace of snaps?

Years ago Thomas Randolph wrote some lines which seem to sum up the philosophy of Reg Bradfield and the Boswell boys.

Stolen sweets are always sweeter.
Stolen kisses much completer.
Stolen looks are nice in chapels.
Stolen, stolen be your apples.

So as Jack Bradfield and Bessie aged, they still earned an honest living on the land. Ron grew up, then the girls went into service, but Bessie in her heart was sad that Reg had taken up with the Boswells in their nightly pursuits.

"You buent averse to utting a rabbit as our Reg brings ya, Missus," Jack would say with a two-toothed grin.

Bessie would sigh as she admitted, "What ud Charlie Baker's widda do avout the firewood he brings her, beside the rabbits?" She often wondered where a certain bit of dressed lamb came from. Did he really escape from the market?

And Jack would look knowing and say, "Stolen sweets."

4

THE WHISTLING PLOUGHMAN

4

The Whistling Ploughman

WHERE THE RAILWAY LINE CROSSED THE AVON NEAR Pershore town the villagers met at a pub known as the Whistling Ploughman. Here the Boswells and the Bradfields mingled with the market gardeners of the black-soiled banks of the river.

The news was mulled over and sieved.

"The Duc d'Aumale's come back to Wood Norton, Caleb," Jack Bradfield announced.

"Yes, in this week's paper, so that's bound to be true." Jack Bradfield pondered a while then said, "I don't know what the French be about. Fust of all they gets shut of they old dukes and princes and such like. And this un comes yer and settles on some of the best of our soil. And then the Frenchmen changes their minds and back whome he goes to France. And now, dal my rags, if they haven't turfed him out again and back he comes to Wood Norton."

"That won't be for long no doubt," Caleb Boswell replied. A well-aimed shot from his tobacco-stained mouth hit the spittoon. "But now the yud man is in residence, there'll be plenty of work on the estate."

Jack looked thoughtfully at the fire and then looking round, making sure that no one from another village should hear said, "Caleb me bwoy, we be well served working for Master Bostock and he does allow us a bit of tater ground, so I be'unt a gwain to work for no French duke." Turning to Sam and Joe Boswell, he added, "Just be careful bwoys with the poaching 'cos they tells me the 'oods be as full of keepers as our village is a drunks on club day."

Sam Boswell found another topic of local interest.

"Sin the paper, you," he said to his brother. "Dammed if our parson unt gone bankrupt, four bob in the pound his paying."

"Now look yer," Caleb said. "Don't thee say a wrong word about him, nor stir up no nast. He's bin a real Christian to me when some of yer brothers went to their graves uth comsumption."

"A good man, I'll warrant," Jack agreed. "And the talk about big bills for communion wine when so few went Sunday mornings unt true, Master Bostock, the warden, says."

"Mind ya, he likes a drop of Maderia, or what they calls it, in the dainty glasses."

"Lors what a night, Landlord," Jack's son Reg announced from the tap room door. "It don't stop to rain, it's bucketing down."

"Oi, it's a few too many spots on one," Caleb replied.

"Fill um up, Landlord, and not too much of a yud on the beer. I wants summat besides froth tonight," Sam said and picking up the paper told the company of trouble at Asum Club.

"Somebody bin mixing the sugar with the sand."

"Why the 'ell dosn't speak in plain English, you?" Caleb butted in. "What dost myun?"

"Well, at the Hannual meeting the books wasn't straight when they met at Beckford Inn and the treasurer has resigned."

Reg Bradfield had walked part of the way from Asum having a railway ticket from the next station.

Joe said, "Surely thee bisn't broke?" But Reg gave him a crafty wink and explained it had saved him the price of a pint, just in case nobody bought him one.

"Much going on in Asum?" Joe asked.

Reg laughed as he came out with one of his usual expressions. "What sights you see when you haven't got your gun."

"Oi, a lot of long-tailed uns in the woods, I'll warrant," Caleb remarked. "Pheasants be out of season, but I udn't like to be un thirty yards off Reg and his muzzle loader."

"No, not that sort of sight, Royality I myuns." Then Reg explained how he had seen a carriage drawn by four slick grey horses come out of the station yard bringing the Duc d'Aumale from the London train.

"That fella at the Hall knows how to drive the four in hand and I never saw such a coach. With the French emblem as decorations. The sound of the coach horn could be heard at the Town Hall, so they says."

Caleb Boswell who had listened for a while as the amber ale flowed down his throat from his quart pot, laughed, almost spilling his beer.

"What's that to grin about like some Cheshire Cat?" Jack Bradfield said, thinking that Caleb was laughing at his son, Reg.

"Just thinking what a difference the Squarson of Lenchwick's transport is—well he *was* the Squarson, one time a day. He's got that shaggy pony as pulls a basket carriage and has a job to get up Hipton Hill. That's Chafey, the Reverend."

The rain cleared and the workers of the river bend made their way home.

Next night the village carrier called at the Ploughman. He went every Wednesday morning to Asum and back to the village in the evening. Jack Turner by name, he drove a fast nag with a covered cart taking market produce to the Smithfield. Jack was well in with Sam and Reg and Joe, selling their rabbits for them, and the few pheasants they poached from Wood Norton woodland.

Jack was careful with game birds out of season after his cart had been stopped and searched by the police at Gypsies Corner.

"Oi, Wednesday morning I was in a bit of a sweat, when the man in blue stopped me aguyn. They be cute, mind," he told the drinkers in the Ploughman, "but I wasn't born yesterday. Thurs no flies on Jack Turner. 'Morning Constable,' I sez. 'I suppose you wants to have a look through my load. Half a minute, though,' I sez, 'Blossom a sweating smartish and hers ready for her bait.' So I fetches the nose bag from the axle and takes it to her and her munches away at the oats and chaff. And the policeman, he has a look in my cyart and all he sees be a feow hampers of apples and rabbits, all legal like."

Under the chaff and oats in Blossom's bag were four pheasants Jack was selling for Joe Boswell. The policeman found nothing amiss in the cart.

Jack Bradfield smiled. He couldn't help smiling, although he knew the risks the young men were taking in the woods. Risks he had warned them of. He turned to Caleb, "If that unt the licker, hiding pheasants in a horse's nose bag. You lives and learns, but honesty's the best policy."

Caleb spluttered across the glowing logs. "Oi, but it keeps you devilish poor."

The carrier then said how he had been through the woods at Wood Norton, "And it's alive with pheasant and Keeper Wasley told me as all the yud men of Europe be coming to shoot in October. And the Duke's got a room in his house twenty eight foot by twenty-four and he and his missus got to give cold lunch to the shooting party on trestle tables. Kings, queens, emperors, dukes—more blue blood than ever bin to Asum town will be at the shoot."

As Joe and Sam and Reg sat open mouthed at the news old Caleb warned them, "Careful now, bwoys."

5

THE ROYAL CURRANT JELLY BOYS

5

The Royal Currant Jelly Boys

IT MIGHT SEEM A BIT SURPRISING TO FIND THE FOURTH son of the deposed King Louis-Philippe of France settled among the two-crop-a-year market gardeners on the alluvial soil by the River Avon. When the Duc d'Aumale first arrived at Wood Norton in 1857, of course, he expected that one day soon he would be called back to his rightful place in a restored French monarchy. Meanwhile he rented the estate from Edward Holland, Squire of Dumbleton, and devoted his days to two things—hunting and shooting. They must have taken a deal of his money, too.

Edward Holland was Asum's last Liberal member of parliament.

He owned that outcrop of Cotswold country, Dumbleton Hill, and could provide pheasant and partridge shoots fit for kings and princes. The Wood Norton coverts surrounded the farmland of the bit of England known as the Lenches, and the Duke acquired shooting rights as well on adjoining land as far afield as Bishampton.

Here he had invited the tenants and yeoman farmers of the Vale to take part in a deer hunt. He had sent letters by his agent, Charles Randall, inviting his guests to breakfast with him at Wood Norton Hall which in those days, back in the eighteen sixties, was little more than a hunting lodge. After breakfast, the invitations ran, "a deer will be loosed before the harriers". It was common but odd practice in Victorian England to loose a fine deer from a cart and have it pursued by that inferior breed of hound, the harrier. In one of their early hymns Tate and Brady refer to this when they adapt a psalm, "As pants the hart for cooling streams when hastened by the chase". The field on that March day was full of men of distinction. Several French princes accompanied the Duke, including his elder brother, the Prince de Joinville and his nephew, the Duc de Chartres. At breakfast the Duc d'Aumale provided an excellent spread. Unfortunately, the complete menu is lost, but all the guests enjoyed the strawberry pie.

Every so often the Duke's fellow French folks let him go back to France and then changed their minds and threw him out again. He bought the Hall at Wood Norton outright in 1872 and when he was in England devoted himself to sport. He hunted regularly with the local fox hounds and also went out after the Cotswold hare.

It's the hunting pink, the ladies' smart habits, and the sleek horses, ridden at full gallop over the Cotswold walls after Renard the Fox, which give glamour to what's known as the chase. But what of the harriers, the Duc d'Aumale's hare hounds?

The Cotswold acres had been divided long ago for fox hunting. Various packs of hounds hunted between age-old boundaries, drawn by parishes brooks and woods. When a hunted fox crossed into another country, a term used to describe their limits, he was safe when the horn of the huntsman called his pack away. So a foreign duke, with a pack of hounds of his own had no option but to hunt the hare. Hare hunting was an older sport, but the field, or followers, were looked upon as an inferior set. The huntsmen who wielded the whip were dressed in sober green jackets with white breeches. The hounds were often mismarked foxhounds, smaller and not so matching. A farmer in his tweeds fitted into the scene with the harriers better than when hunting the fox.

Hares were plentiful in the late nineteenth century on those bleak limestone hills. No doubt many Cotswold men followed on foot to see the Duc d'Aumale's pack harry and catch the Cotswold hare. Hares have a habit of keeping to their own territory. They run in circles, around a few fields, so by standing on a knoll or "knolp", as a Cotswold man would say, the chase could be watched without a lot of walking. How different Sally the Hare is from Renard the Fox, who will run with the wind behind his brush, taking a straight line from covert to covert.

When the motley crowd met in a farmyard, much as in Shakespeare's day, the Duke led his pack with Ron Bradfield as his huntsman. They found their first hare in Mr Cook's turnip field. Hares often make for a farm gate or perhaps a narrow bridle gate when chased from one field to another. Long runs were seldom on those hills. With ears laid low, using her hind legs like a miniature kangaroo, Sally gave the harriers a good run. Sometimes she would run through a flock of those giant Cotswold sheep and put the pack off scent.

One must wonder how the Duc d'Aumale became such a successful Master of the Harriers. Charles Cook, no doubt, lent him a wrinkle or two about how to run a pack of hare hounds on those Cotswold hills. Old Charles Cook of Taddinton reconciled being a true yeoman of England and a tenant of the French Duke very well. He was a man of many parts, a breeder of excellent horses and valiant sons, hill farmer of repute, rhyme writer, a dispenser of fine port wine and he knew and enjoyed all the best things a successful agriculturist and good sportsman could have with the Duke as his landlord.

A magazine of the day recalls how Charles entertained the foreign gentry, who were affectionately known as the Royal Currant Jelly Boys. The hunt breakfast over and the toasts drunk, Charles Cook rose to his feet to make an address.

"My noble princes of France, earls, dukes etcetera. I feel honoured by your presence here today to accept the hospitality of a British farmer and hunt a Cotswold hare. When I first saw you French gentlefolks riding over the wall bang in front of a well-mounted field I was told that you were frog eaters. 'Never,' I said, 'Never. No French chaps could sit down and ride like that to hounds.' My Lords, dukes and princes, I have been truly converted from the error of my ways. Now I'm prepared to back you on horseback against any Englishman over these Cotswold walls. My noble guests, I sincerely trust that that fellow Napoleon won't abdicate just yet. 'Cos why? We should lose you, and it will be a bad day for us all. May we forever see your horses' footmarks on our land. We are proud of our royal exiles, for we have learnt to respect and honour the brave and true sons of France."

Then he turned to his son Tom and bade him bring the biggest of the silver cups he had won at steeple chasing on the Cotswold, and filled it to the brim with champagne.

"Now," said Charles, handing the great two-handled goblet to the Duke, "please oblige me by drinking out of my son's winnings in your own country's wine. Then we ull have a little hollering."

Charles Randall, the Duke's agent, was a remarkable man, a nineteenth century public relations officer. He smoothed out any creases that might develop between a pretender to the throne of France and the conservative tenantry on the estate. And indeed the Duke's natural modesty and gregariousness made him popular with his tenants.

There is little doubt that had Charles Randall had a full say in the farming of the land, he would have seen to it that the tenants worked more efficiently. It was not to be. The Duke, though a supporter of the Asum Agricultural Society, was lenient. His rents were paid but Charles Randall, as one of Britain's leading agriculturists, must have been disappointed that his prime job was to see that the coverts were stocked.

The Duc d'Aumale relied on Charles Randall and Charles Randall relied on Keeper Wasley, or Neighbour Wasley as he was known to the men on the estate, to see that a good lot of pheasants were presented flying above the guns at the shoot. Shoots were often on a Saturday. The Duke's coverts were literally alive with game, corn-fed by Neighbour and his under keepers until October 1st. October 1st, being the first shoot of the season, was looked upon in the same way as the Glorious Twelfth of August on the grouse moors.

There was more to a shoot at Wood Norton when the Duc d'Aumale was in residence than a day with the guns. It was a kind of ritual. Neighbour Wasley mustered together the men and boys of the estate and neighbouring villages to act as beaters. As the visiting kings, queens and emperors of Europe met the landed gentry of the Vale for a drink at the Hall, Mr Randall was instructed to tell the noblemen where in the line of guns they were to stand and wait for the birds. I would say that this would be a difficult task to perform, or did they draw lots? You see, the men in the middle of the line of guns were in a better position, as they would normally have more birds flying over them than the men at each end of the line. Each beater carried an ash or nut stick to beat the scrub trees to disturb the pheasants so that as the army of men and boys advanced towards the gentry, the birds fled ahead of them. A distant crackling of undergrowth, perhaps half a mile away, and Wasley's voice would be heard shouting to his line of beaters to keep their sticks moving on the right or the left. Every blackberry bush was combed by Wasley's dogs so that the pheasants could not cower under cover. If a fox was disturbed and ran with outstretched brush towards the guns he would frighten the pheasants and make them take wing across the ride of grass opening between the woods. This was unpleasing to Wasley for the birds were too many together for the guns to deal with. The battue went on like a continuous barrage until the last bird took flight, making its way to the next covert of woodland, only to fall in the ride, victim to the guns.

The gentry had a code of conduct never to shoot low towards the beater. They picked their bird as it came over and could not swing their guns across the line but only shoot at the pheasants which winged over them. Artificial as it seems, there was a great deal of skill in shooting birds from some rides. Reg Bradfield tells how the Duc d'Aumale could hit pheasants in a valley-like ride, between two wooded small hills. Here the birds looked like starlings as they soared across, just in reach of the shot from the guns.

Every duke, king and gentleman had an experienced man to load his guns. The guns were in pairs. One held loaded by the sportsman, another by the loader who handed it to him when he had emptied both barrels of powder and shot from gun number one. The Duke himself had an experienced loader; none other than a junior keeper. Every time the shooters moved on from one drive to another, one of the bigger boys on the estate followed with the game cart while the beaters picked up the fallen birds and the dogs retrieved the ones that had been winged. The ritual of the shoots at the Hall was rigid. Everyone knew their place. At lunchtime the foreign dukes and princes went to Neighbour Wasley's house where, in the long room there, they had a cold meal and a drink. Outside on iron stays flew all the flags of the countries of Europe from which they had come.

The extravagance of the Duke's pheasant shoots reminds me of a saying of later years which shows how pheasant rearing is a sport for the rich and the birds for the table are dearly bought: "Up gets seven and six pence (the cost of rearing the bird). Bang goes two pence (the cost of the cartridge). And down comes half a crown (the value of the pheasant)." Racing is called the sport of kings. Perhaps shooting should be called the sport of dukes?

6

ON THE BLACK SOIL

6

On the Black Soil

THE LAND AROUND WOOD NORTON STRETCHES WEST OF Evesham in the bow of Shakespeare's Avon as far as the ruins of Asum Abbey. The local people describe its soil as being black as your hat. In its richness grow cabbages, plums and unbeatable strawberries.

This is the land which was stained with the blood of Simon de Montfort and his men in the slaughter of 1265, but its continuing fertility is usually attributed to the monks of Asum Abbey who, some say, were the first gardeners of the Vale. It could be, also, that the flooding of the river gave the land some of its special qualities, before the Avon was made navigable and the locks built by a certain Lord Sandys.

Here, after the Birmingham railway from Asum opened in 1864, the fruit and early cabbages flowed on the iron roads to London, Birmingham and the North. Men with donkeys and carts loaded the trucks in village sidings besides at the busy centre of Asum, where the market auctioneer had to compete with the braying of these strong but stubborn animals.

Charles Woolen lived in a thatched house along the Waterside with his wife Emma. In the great flood late in the century the water reached the landing. Charles looked through the little dormer window in the thatch and saw in the early light of dawn the flotsam and jetsam of the Vale swirling in mid stream towards the Severn Vale. The water had risen in the night and his wife feared they were doomed.

"We be in God's hands, Emma," he said. "And he ull turn the tide."

When Charles looked at his watch next, it was half past seven, time he had done an hour's work. But scanning the flooded road he noticed that the water mark on a tree trunk opposite was a couple of inches lower then it had been half an hour before. So the water was ebbing.

At nine a boat arrived rowed by a fellow market gardener, loaded with fresh loaves of bread. The boatman wielded a long pitching shuppick used for pitching hay, and spiked the loaves on the end in order to hoist them up to the Woolens' bedroom window ledge.

After the flood went down the smell of river water stayed in their house until late summer. It seemed odd to see the whale's jawbone smeared with river mud and still standing, forming an archway to the pleasure grounds by the riverside. No doubt Charles and Emma thought of Noah and how he escaped. You see, Charles and Emma were God-fearing folk. They saw the miracles of nature and prized their black fertile sod.

At Asum on their holding, known as the Charity, the Woolens grew a marvellous strain of brussels sprouts. It's true Charles double-dug his land, and was generous with the guano fertiliser which was being shipped from Peru, but his sprouts were as big and hard as his knarled fists.

Plum picking time in the Vale.

Among the strawberry rows.

A pea-picking party rests its backs.

Down by the riverside Charles grew his osiers for hamper-making, and on wet days he and his man, Ned, mended their hampers which held his produce for market. Ned had worked as a lamp-lighter for the gas works. He said that he didn't mind lighting them, but was nervous about douting the lamps up Donnybrook, over the river. His last lamp to dout was at the churchyard gate. The night seemed very dark when this one went out. He declared that he had met the Holy Ghost dressed in white among the tombstones. It turned out to be Charles Woolen's donkey which had got out from the orchard at the back of his house.

The final blow came for Ned and his work with the pole douting the gas lamps when Sergeant Booth flung his arms around his waist just as the light went out.

So Ned finished his night work and picked sprouts for the Woolens. He got paid every Saturday and Charles Woolen's small boy, Stephen, was always sent out of the hovel at the Charity while it happened. But whipping around to the back of the shed, he could see Ned rubbing one half sovereign in the palm of his hand for his week's work.

Stephen was seven years old and called after his Grandad who had been a gardener near Wood Norton. When he died the tombstone of this old Vale gardener was carved with plums, pears and apples, encircled by peas in the pod with pods bursting, cauliflowers and everything this land produced.

Charles was not content with sprouts alone as his speciality. He travelled by horse and spring cart to the Blenheim country around Woodstock, Chalbury and Kidlington and bought orchards of fruit on the trees—Blenheims and sourings.

He employed more labour, and trucked his fruit at Chalbury where he saw the longest runner bean he had ever seen. Asking the cottager for some seed, he was given six beans which he planted in the spring on the Charity. The pods were just the same length as his pot hampers and straight and sound. None were picked for eating, but were harvested for seed the first two or three years, until he had enough seed to plant half an acre.

He topped the market making a record price.

Every wholesaler and merchant was eager to buy beans like Charles' to display on the shop-fronts of Manchester, Birmingham and London. However there was one drawback. The yield was not heavy. All the winter Charles Woolen pondered how he could improve this. He crossed them with a high yielding bean of moderate size.

The result is still talked of in the Vale today, for didn't Charles Woolen make a thousand pounds out of beans in three years?

Then the strain reverted.

Charles had an accident as he brought a load of straw to Charity on his cart. As he slid down the rope holding the load, his horse moved on and the wheel crushed his leg. He lay with a box of sand around the injured limb for twelve months, then died leaving a big bill to pay the doctor.

Emma was undaunted. She still grew the famous Woolen strain of sprouts, brewed her beer, made her cider, taking on more labour, including a man who worked part-time for her called Kick Pudding, and sold steaming lardy cakes and buns and bananas from a basket truck on three iron wheels.

"Ripe banawnaws," he called as he travelled the cobbled streets of Asum, a character who lived on and on to an age as ripe as his bananas.

I can remember Kick Pudding, his steel-rimmed glasses and his broken wicker truck. What an opinion he had of himself! In fact, he was a self-educated man, a student of Darwin and an uncompromising atheist, and that took some pluck in the nineteenth century.

As he walked he quoted—and misquoted—pieces of wisdom as he thought fit for the company he ankle tapped with his truck on the narrow pavements or cobbled drive entrance. A favourite of his, if women were shopping and got in his way, was, "Women are deceitful above all things and desperately wicked."

Mrs Woolen grew her crops and harvested her crops as well as any man in the Vale. She had no need to soak her pot hampers in the well to cheat on the weight and her sprouts weighed like lead.

Working with Kick Pudding part-time at the Charity was Monkey McCoy, a man who roughed it, as it was said, sleeping in the hovel. He drove the workhouse horse and cart around the town selling firewood, chopped and split by the thousands of tramps who passed that way. Monkey McCoy arrived with the vagrants, but stayed in Asum. Why was he called Monkey? Have you studied the apes at the zoo? Monkey was unfortunate in that he was missing when good looks were doled out. His withered face and reddened eyes with snub-nosed open nostrils and his protruding bottom lip made him look a brother to the monkey tribe. His long arms and big hands stretched well below his knees. A frightening man, to be pitied. Yet he made capital out of his animal appearance, as he ploughed head forward through Asum streets. For one penny Monkey would pull an ugly face to a crowd in the Saturday market place. An even more frightening grimace was twopence.

Of course, Monkey was of low intelligence, but he did lend Kick Pudding some weight in support of the Darwinian theory of evolution.

To cap it all, Emma Woolen employed a man off the Cotswold known as Tommy the Book. He toured the Vale villages on Sundays, helping a band of open-air preachers. No doubt a sincere man, and a worker but again a man with an imperfection. Even kings may have impediments of speech.

One Sunday he announced the hymn: "Hymn number ticty tix, ti tankey tongs and tolos, is that tumbody do."

Then he sang, "It that tumbody you number ticty tix."

So Emma went bravely on with her holding. Life was hard, but fair at the Charity. At half past three the men were out picking the strawberries, groping in the half light of dawn. They worked hard and were never expected to straighten their backs, as they hoed the strawberries or cabbages, except when the land was wet and the soil stuck to the hoe plate. Every man kept a piece of wood shaped like a knife tucked in the yorks, or straps, under the knee of his cord trousers. These cleaning pegs were known as "minute wasters", for no master or mistress could complain if one of the men straightened his back to clean a hoe plate with the wooden peg.

Emma killed four pigs a year, so the whitewashed kitchen wall were hung with the yellow flitches of cured bacon. Ned records the best picture—the large frying pan, hung by its half round handle from the pot hooks, the slices of thick fattish bacon curled up and having a look at Emma, as she turned them with the bone-handled carving fork before putting them in a meat tin on the side. Twelve new-laid hen eggs would sizzle and splutter over the fire between the hobs. There'd be fried bread and home-made cottage loaves, and a crock of cider from Emma's orchard.

The strawberry pickers breakfasted quite as well as the Queen who was still on the throne of Britain.

Then Emma was taken ill and young Doris Bradfield came over from Carrants View Cottage to look after the household. The Woolen family were still young, and Emma needed a foreman, so Philip Bradfield lived in at the Charity and managed the holding.

As she lay in bed with the family gathered around her, Emma said, "You folk think I am going to die, don't you? Well I'll be at work in a fortnight. Get off all of you and pick those strawberries and cut the hearted cabbage for market."

The doctor spoke soft and low telling the family it was a matter of time. The patient had a serious internal condition.

"I'm tougher than you think," Emma told her sons.

She was right, too. She was out in a fortnight and lived to be ninety-one.

7

ASUM'S NEW ARMY

7

Asum's New Army

General Booth's influence spread across Britain like a tidal wave of religious revival. It was different from earlier revivals in Wales and such. The General's message was that of a social gospel. "No good talking to a man about his soul if his belly is empty," he often said. The Salvation Army established itself in Asum in the eighteen eighties and straight away found a problem to tackle—drink.

The men of the black soil were mostly little master men with five or twenty acres. Their work hours had no limit. It's true, established families like the Woolens could stand a time of depressed prices and see their plums rot on the trees. Other growers had few assets. They depended on a willing working wife and children, and a donkey to take their produce to market or station in a cart. The land was precious so Neddy the donkey grazed the grass verges in the town, sharing the surplus carrots and parsnips with the family pig. In wet awkward times or when the market was at a low ebb the gardeners congregated in their hovels, sheds of brick with fireplaces and barrels of home-made plum jerkum, parsnip wine, rhubarb wine—the lot. They would have a session lasting a week or more and drink to drown their sorrows. I can understand the logic of it all in a land where no one really cared for the struggling or the poor.

The Salvation Army was formed in Asum Town Hall and attracted this very element of the Vale society. But General Booth's rules were strict. Was he a dictator? I suppose so, but he was a dictator for good. If an ordinary working chap joined he signed "The Articles of War". They included total abstinence from intoxicating liquor, no smoking or taking snuff, no attendance at theatres or football matches, no swearing, dances or cards. Sunday was to be kept strictly for worship and open-air meetings, and any form of work was forbidden.

Of course, men who had signed the Articles of War slipped up sometimes. Behind the blue and gold uniform or the red jersey men were human and still open to temptation.

The Army's rules were rigid, but did not rule out a market gardener shooting the starlings on his strawberry patch on Sunday mornings. A blind eye was turned to this, but when one soldier was caught shooting a pheasant on his holding out of season *and* on a Sunday he was suspended from the band for a month. This also happened to a friend of my Uncle Fred's who made up a couch grass fire on Sunday morning.

The advent of the Salvation Army was however the beginning of the end of Victorian complacency. At last the worship of God became Catholic in a real sense. A door was opened in the barracks for the verminous tramp, the vagrant, the drunkard. No one was barred because of the state of their clothes. In fact, these outcasts were the folk the Army threw out a lifeline to.

It's true the churches of the town had their various charities to help the poor and unfortunate, but the Army reached out further still to the lice-infested lodging houses and drew the people from here and from the pubs they could ill afford to frequent to the barracks.

One can talk glibly of instant conversion from everything distasteful in life to a state of honest respectability. But it happened. The Salvation Army, as I learnt from Dad and my Uncle Fred, certainly influenced their conversion. The evidence is without dispute. Perhaps the change was more apparent, simply because so many were often at such a low ebb before their conversion. The Salvation Army offered simple compassion to people, however out of time they were with their fellow men. The music of the band and the forthright expressions of faith acted as a balm to the needy.

The way the Salvation Army was accepted in Asum was mixed. It was bound to be; even Wesley and Whitfield disagreed about open-air preaching. One great champion of the Army was the Vicar himself. This is surprising when the Wesleyans were not willing to support them to the full. One Asum newspaper was all for the new movement in the town. The other took every opportunity to criticise the men in blue uniform.

So the first officer came to break new ground among the fruit orchards and cabbage fields around Asum and Wood Norton.

Uncle Fred was a young market gardener. He signed the Articles of War and, being musical, took his stand among the newly-formed band. Uncle Fred had a strong sense of humour. He found a funny story wherever he went, a good quality to have when opposition was strong. He told me how he marched smartly with the band to take part in an open-air meeting one Saturday night at a notorious spot known as the four corners of hell. It was the junction of four narrow streets, flanked with three public houses and some common lodging houses, and it was here the opposition attacked, in the shape of a skeleton force primed with free drink by the opponents of the Army. They threw eggs and then flour at the band as they played, and Uncle Fred had only just saved up for his new uniform.

But don't let us underestimate the vigour of the women of the four corners. As Uncle Fred was under attack his Aunt Harriet watched from her cottage window overlooking the pavement. Aunt Harriet was made of stern stuff and leaping into the road in bonnet and shawl, her long auburn hair flying, she used her fists like a man and stood in the ring willing to take the attackers on two at a time.

These serious encounters were infrequent however and got more so when a certain sergeant of the police marched in front of the band from High Street to the barracks. Picture the earliest of these bands marching awkwardly down High Street, the man with the flag close behind the heels of Sergeant Farman, Uncle Fred with his wry smile and twinkling eye struggling with the huge G trombone, an instrument with a handle to reach the slide. These were the recruits General Booth called to the colours of Blood and Fire.

As the euphonium player stepped along those cobbled streets the youths of the town threw parched peas down the horn from the pavement. A cross-eyed soldier tried playing a cornet, then gave up to beat the bass drum. Uncle Fred said he needed a cross-eyed cornet. At the Town Hall the police sergeant turned left, followed by the band, past the Volunteer Inn. The cross-eyed chap on the big bass drum was so intent in beating hell out of the leather, he marched alone into the market place. Here was a mixture of a deep spiritual uplift and entertainment.

In the market place on those never to be forgotten Saturday nights the townsfolk packed in between the Town Hall and the Round House. The Army was being accepted and music so different from that of church or chapel filled that square. "Why should the Devil have all the best tunes," General Booth had declared and the song writers at the London headquarters were putting the Gospel message to music hall songs.

The Evesham gardeners who joined the General's colours prospered. Not just because they had accepted the Good News of the Gospel, but because they came to terms with life and many reversed their priorities. The weeks of useless sessions on the plum jerkum were over. In the little brick hovels where they kept their tools on their smallholdings wet days were spent in a different way. Far from the houses and shops Uncle Fred told me how often he heard a recruit in the band practise on his instrument. Discord of course at first, but they improved.

One Friday night at band practice a bandsman who played a bombardon kept on putting his comrades out of time by playing an odd note.

"That note's not in the music book," the bandmaster said. "You are wrong, you know, George."

Puzzled, George showed his book to the bandmaster. The bandmaster examined the music, frowned, rubbed the page with his thumb and the note rubbed off. It was a spot where a fly had left a message.

Sucking oranges close to the Army band ring was one trick some of the Asum lads got up to in that market square. It's pretty difficult, Uncle told me, to use the lips and tongue on a wind instrument when someone sucks an orange alongside, because it makes the mouth water and then the notes can't come clear.

Let no one say these bandsmen were not sincere. Uncouth, ignorant and knowing little of the outside world, they intended nevertheless to make Asum a better place to live in. Not just on Sundays but every day. Teas and suppers were organised for the old folk. A young soldier whom I knew in the band told me of the poverty up Donnybrook on the other side of Asum river. Here he sang "Break the News to Mother" when Ladysmith was relieved, and women in hurden or sacking aprons wept and threw pennies to him. The following year the band played the Death March up and down the High Street the evening that Queen Victoria died. When the *Titanic* sank some years later they did the same thing.

What of the witness of these early Salvationists? I do believe that the understanding dry humour of these men took them a long way to winning the support of the majority of Asum folk in the early days. One officer was blessed, if one can say blessed, with a powerful voice, and he bellowed out the message of the Gospel. A favourite cry of his was, "He's alive!" A butcher mimicked him and called back from his shop, "He's alive!" The officer turned quick as a flash and answered, "Don't say that, my friend. You won't sell your meat if it's alive." I hesitate to say how these men gave their testimony. It was, as one would expect, crude. One bandsman, who grew a long beard below his cornet, was understood by his friends, but his words were very muddled.

"Well friends," he would start, "before I joined the Army I hadn't got a rag to my back or a shoe to my foot. Now I got, look ya, pony and cart, two bicycles all paid for, my wife's my own, and my kids my own. If you don't repent thurs hards times ahead. You ull be working for the Devil digging taters by the bushel with a wooden pick and shovel on the turnpike road. What should you do, friends, if one morning you woke up and found yourself dead in the bottom of the bottomless pit of hell? Where should you be then?"

I have been brought up with these men and their sons and know the depth of their belief in something to live for.

One bandsman had served in India and was carried away as he testified in the ring. "All the way to Calcutta our Saviour went for us all." Quite a step from Calcutta to Calvary, but I'm sure he meant well.

Around the ring on these Saturday nights in the market place the rough and tumble of Asum drifted from the pubs. Sam and Joe Boswell were fellow market gardeners and friends of my Uncle Fred. It was his lasting regret that he almost persuaded them to join the band. Almost but not quite. The trouble was, they had so much to give up.

8

TROUBLE IN THE WOODS

8

Trouble in the Woods

SAM AND JOE BOSWELL, HAVING REFUSED TO JOIN Uncle Fred in the Salvation Army, took over a holding near the green, stopping towards the River Avon at Asum. It was on this green they met Doris and Kate Bradfield at the Asum Mop or hiring fair. Both girls were hired for one year's domestic service in Asum town, while Sam and Joe courted them.

It seemed that Sam and Joe had left off their poaching ways for a while. Jack and Bessie Bradfield, now old and past work, were glad when their daughters agreed to marry the Boswell boys.

"They be steady now, Missus," Jack said to Bessie, as they sat in Carrants View cottage.

"Ah, a bit a land ull make um steadier still, now they be married."

Both daughters had baby boys within twelve months and Joe's wife Kate had a little girl the next year. The families worked hard on the old Abbey land.

Those Saturday nights in the market place still sounded with the music of the Salvation Army band. Uncle Fred spoke often to Sam and Joe as they listened on the outside edge of the ring, and when the soldiers of Booth collected at the Jolly Gardeners pub the Boswells gave generously. I'm sure these two brothers were attracted to the Army.

A year or two passed in the life of the Asum gardeners. By this time Caleb and his wife had died leaving Jack and Bessie Bradfield lonely, apart from young Phil, at their cottage.

Lovely Hill became a friend of Sam and Joe. He was much younger than they, working as a stoker at the gas works and, being the only son of Tom the Ferret, poaching was in his blood. For hadn't Tom the Ferret poached the Cotswolds as a travelling man from Chipping Sodbury to Stratford-upon-Avon from Michaelmas until Lady Day?

What a pity that Sam and Joe joined Lovely Hill and that they started netting rabbits with the long nets and lurcher dogs in the precarious Wood Norton woods. As the autumn leaves fell Sam, Joe and Lovely Hill grew more crafty and venturesome as they silently combed the drives between the Wood Norton trees for rabbits. For by now the Duke, or his bailiff to be exact, had doubled the number of keepers and night watchmen, and the woods at night were entangled with trip wires fixed to spring guns. Although doubtfully legal, it is said that Keeper Wasley also set the dreaded mantrap.

Yes, it was a challenge for men to be in the Duc d'Aumale's woods on those autumn nights of 1889. The night of November 9th was dry, the wind was light and the moon was full. One wonders why experienced men of the woods like Sam, Joe and Lovely Hill chose this night to take out their nets and dogs. The netting of rabbits is more certain to produce a good bag when the wind blows fresh in the face and takes with it the noise of every

The Duc d'Aumale.

The Duc d'Orleans.

The Golden Gates at Wood Norton.

stick cracked under the feet of men and dogs. In the Jolly Gardeners, where only the Black Bridges over the railway separated Asum from Wood Norton woods, Sam, Joe and Lovely Hill passed the evening on the wooden settle with Mary Johnson, Joe Beard and Tom Spragg, drinking cool amber cider from the apples of the Vale. Cider slightly cloudy from the barrel, strong drink indeed, fetched in crock mugs by Fanny Moyle, the barmaid.

"Pity Phil Bradfield unt with us tonight," Sam remarked to his brother. Phil had got a good net and a useful lurcher.

Joe grinned and mouthed one word, "Metheglin."

The brothers had called for Phil to find him lying paralytic on the rag rug in front of the fire after a day drinking the mead from his father's bees.

"Sensible as a Christian, he was," Joe told Tom Spragg. "Sensible in the yud I mean, but his legs wouldn't carry him."

The little company of Asum market gardeners and the women played cards around the fire until closing time.

Tom Spragg was a two-faced character, not to be trusted, a nosey listener to other men's talk, Judas fashion. He didn't like Sam and Joe Boswell or Lovely Hill. Although he lived in one of the Duke's cottages, he no longer worked on the estate.

It appears that Sam, Joe and Lovely crossed the Black Bridges soon after midnight and walked with their dogs and long nets to comb the rides between the woods at a place high up above the Duke's house known as Tunnel Hill.

The first draw was made. As the dogs worked the rabbits towards the net, Joe and Sam took the entangled animals from the net, while Lovely walked the woods with the lurcher dogs.

Keeper Wasley had warned all the under keepers never to walk the woods alone at night, because of the poachers from Asum. Fred Stephens who lived in a keeper's cottage on Hipton Hill was young, strong and cared for no one. He did his beat across Tunnel Hill without waiting for Wasley. The men were just bagging their game to make a quick get-away when foolishly, yet doing his duty, he tackled the Boswell brothers and Lovely Hill.

During the fight Stephens was seriously injured and lay for a time across an ash stool as if dead, before he came too sufficiently to blow his whistle, which was heard by keeper Wasley as he walked the next coverts with one of his under men. Keeper Wasley took Fred Stephens to Dr Haynes, while the poachers arrived home at Merstow Green at three o'clock.

Twelve days later Fred Stephens died.

9

THE MURDER OF FRED STEPHENS

9

The Murder of Fred Stephens

At the Asum Sessions the bench consisted of the landed gentry of the Vale. The Boswell brothers were charged with the wilful murder of Frederick Stephens. They pleaded not guilty. Police Sergeant Turner gave evidence that when he arrested the men early on November 10th, he found poaching materials and sticks at Joe Boswell's house. Neighbour Wasley head keeper for the Duc d'Aumale said in court that Stephens was brought to him at three a.m. on November 10th and said he had been attacked by three poachers. He was covered with blood and Wasley took Stephens to Dr Haynes.

Dr Haynes said that Stephens was bleeding freely and that on

November 12th he removed a portion of depressed bone from his skull with the aid of a colleague from Birmingham. It measured four inches by two and a half inches. Stephens was conscious during the surgery. Dr Haynes said that the fracture was in his opinion the result of blows from a blunt instrument or kicks. He had never seen a patient recover from such head damage. He said that he examined the elder Boswell in the cells and found bite marks on his fingers.

It does seem a miracle that nearly a hundred years ago, in a time of elementary surgery, Doctor Haynes kept Stephens alive for twelve days. I recall my Dad telling me how his father fell from a wheat rick to the stone rickyard floor and fractured his skull in about 1889. Yes, they took him home on a bed of straw in a muck cart. A cart without springs over the rough wheel ruts of our village street. Our doctor kept the unconscious old man in bed, his head between sandbags. And he lived.

It does strike me that perhaps if Dr Haynes had been allowed to keep Stephens still and he had not been badgered by the police, he may have lived. But Stephens was dead and two men stood in the dock.

Joe Beard, who was considered a doubtful witness and a notorious liar, said that while the police were with the Boswell brothers, Lovely Hill climbed the wall from Merstow Green into the brewery yard near the Trumpet.

Sam Boswell replied, "Coulds't *thee* jump that wall? Thee bist a liar. It's fifteen foot high and impossible."

In Joe Boswell's house Sergeant Turner found a walking stick, Stephens' hat, two pieces of string which were used as dog slips, also six hazel sticks, like rick pegs, two feet long.

Superintendent Kemp turned to Keeper Wasley and asked him if these were net pegs. Wasley replied, "Yes, Sir."

Joe Boswell said he knew nothing of dog slips and the nets belonged to a neighbour who caught rabbits in a wood pile. A net was found near Battleton Bridge, which Joe recognised as one belonging to Lovely Hill.

Sergeant Turner said he also found three bludgeons in Joe Boswell's house. Joe Boswell repeatedly denied hitting Stephens with a stick. He said he had never used an unlawful weapon, only his fist, and he wasn't guilty. Stephens, he was sure, had fallen and hit his head on an ash stool. The Police did find blood on an ash stool.

Sam Boswell said he was out with a man named David Hirons and called him as a witness. Then Sam asked if he could call his missus, but the Chairman of the Bench refused. But Sam had to admit that he held Stephens by the throat to make him loose his hand which Stephens was biting so hard.

The court adjourned for more witnesses to give evidence.

At the resumed hearing Joe Boswell described how Stephens hit his brother over the eye and then Lovely Hill hit Stephens on the top of the head with a knobbed stick. The stick was produced in court; the knob was as big as a man's fist. Joe described what happened when Lovely Hill hit Stephens. "He hit him so hard I said, 'Good God, thee hast killed him!' I said, 'Come on, chaps, we ull have some more after us.' And we ran all the way to Merstow Green. When we got there there were dogs barking, then the police came and Hill escaped."

Keeper Wasley, called to give evidence again, admitted that Stephens should not have parted from the other under keeper.

When asked by the Chairman about an invention of Messrs Wilder of Birmingham for giving light on dark nights, Keeper Wasley said it gave an instant light and he used it.

"It looks like a short stick and all that's necessary is to strike it against the foot and wave it in the air and it gives a very good light and the keeper can see who is about. Midnight marauders can stand anything better than light."

The Chairman thanked Neighbour Wasley for this piece of information.

Tom Spragg in evidence said that he was in the Jolly Gardeners on November 9th and that he heard Sam Boswell say to Joe, "If anyone comes to tackle us we will knock his bloody yud off."

Sam answered straight away saying that Spragg was a liar who once worked for the Duke and wanted his job back.

Fanny Moyle said she never heard this threat, but the men were together at cards.

Joe spoke up and said, "Tell the truth lad," to Spragg and, turning to the bench, asked whether there would be funds to prosecute Spragg for perjury. "Cos he says he was there when we were arrested and it's lies. He's trying to creep back to his job."

When the Chairman announced that the Boswell brothers would be commited for trial at the Worcester Assizes, Joe answered, "Thank you Sir, but I have a request to make."

The bench agreed to listen to the younger brother.

"I am going to leave a small family behind," he said. "I hope the police will allow em a little till we come whoame again."

"What for?" the Chairman demanded.

"Victuals, Sir."

"That's nothing to do with us."

"They can't live on nothing."

"You should have thought about that before," said the Chairman of the Bench. Wiping his eyes, Joe was allowed to see his wife as he left the dock.

This was an odd winding up of Petty Sessions, for surely the Boswells were still innocent in the sight of the law until the jury's verdict at Worcester.

It was all beginning to look like a foregone conclusion and in his Sunday sermon the Vicar of Asum quoted John Bradford's famous words as he saw a man on his way to the gallows, "There but for the grace of God goes John Bradford." True there were probably some poachers among his flock, so perhaps the word was in season.

10

THE SEARCH FOR LOVELY HILL

10

The Search for Lovely Hill

AT THE SOUTH END OF ASUM TOWN HALL THE GAOL HAD stood as a place of punishment for many many years. Joe and Sam were confined in the cells there, but exercised in the yard near the Green which is nowadays the site of a ladies' convenience. A high Cotswold stone wall stood between them and the world outside. It was the custom of the Salvation Army band to play in the market place near the wall.

That Sunday afternoon after the Chairman of Asum bench had passed the final decision on to Worcester Assizes, Uncle Fred was there with his G trombone, and just a wall between the Army and the prisoners who had so often been on the outside ring at open-air services on Sundays. The Salvation Army officer stood among his men. The bandmaster waved his baton and about twenty-five to thirty of the band played "Jesus Lover of my Soul'. Men and women of the Vale wept when the officer gave out the third verse, "Other refuge have I none, Hangs my helpless soul on thee, Leave, ah leave me not alone, Still support and comfort me."

Uncle Fred, whose sky-blue eyes saw most things, stood with his back to the little saddler's shop on the market place. He was a bit elevated there. He needed to be, as he was not a lot bigger than his instrument. And over the wall he spotted Joe Boswell exercising in the prison yard. Joe, whom he had known from youth, stopped and looked at Uncle Fred and with his two hands clasped tightly around his throat he shouted, "Fred, it's going to be the rope."

Meanwhile the search went on for Alfred Hill, known as Lovely Hill. All seaports were watched, especially Liverpool, for it was expected that he might flee to Canada.

One weakness Lovely had and that was singing in pubs when he had had some beer. Included in his repertoire was Will Oliver's pathetic ballad, "Don't put my father's picture up for sale". A rumour came to Asum that Lovely Hill had been heard singing it in a Birmingham pub.

P.C. Charles Bayliss had been at Merstow Green school with Lovely Hill and knew him well. So the Asum superintendent sent Bayliss to Birmingham to visit the pubs and lodging houses and find Hill, even if it was like looking for a needle in a haystack. After a while an Inspector Stroud was also sent to Birmingham to help in the search.

For over a month these two officers walked the streets that cold wet December of 1889. News came that Hill had been heard singing his song in a Dartmouth Street pub. P.C. Bayliss arrived minutes late. So once more Lovely Hill gave the police the slip. Inspector Stroud developed the influenza through the nightly vigil he kept in the back streets of Birmingham. But like a true British copper he kept going, accompanied by young Bayliss.

A few days later Bayliss and Stroud went to Windsor Street gas works where it was believed that Hill was employed as a coke runner. P.C. Bayliss disguised himself as a workman and blacked his face with soot like the others. This son of an Asum market gardener was a brave lad, as with grimed face he worked a while in the gas works. He soon recognized Lovely Hill among the other men, and the police moved in. Bayliss put a hand on Lovely's shoulder and said, "Come on, lad. I've been looking for Lovely Hill and you are him."

Immediately Hill kicked Bayliss, but Stroud and a Birmingham police officer closed in and took him handcuffed to Moor Street police station.

Hill then admitted his name and that he had been living with a Mrs O'Brian under the name of Jim Weeks. Her address was Dartmouth Street and she told P.C. Bayliss that Hill had been working a late shift at the gas works until ten o'clock in the evening. He was chatty, she said, and played with her children. Every Wednesday he went shopping in the Market Hall. He never mentioned poaching and smoked a pipe.

But tragedy seemed ever present in this hunt for the killer of Fred Stephens. Inspector Stroud was rushed to hospital in Birmingham that day with pneumonia. The constant beat he had done in wet clothes in the city streets had made him a very sick man. He died two days later.

When the Birmingham police sent a telegram to Asum that Lovely Hill was at Moor Street another officer went up on the Midland train, Sergeant Sid Wasley, a brother of the Duke's head keeper.

The train with the two officers and Hill was due to arrive at Asum Station at six fifty, after leaving Birmingham New Street at five o'clock. It's just a thought that this train ran until the line was closed recently. In fact the five o'clock from New Street was the last train to run on that line.

As the carriage door was unlocked a short thick-set man appeared in fustian clothes, wearing a poke cap, handcuffed to an officer in plain clothes, Sergeant Wasley. As passers-by shouted "Hello", Lovely Hill waved to them. A cab waited to take this begrimed man to Asum police station where a knot of Lovely's friends greeted him. The prisoner just replied, "Hello, chaps," and he was soon safely locked up in the Town Hall.

After the hearing at Asum Sessions Lovely Hill was committed for trial at Worcester Assizes along with Sam and Joe Boswell.

The months the brothers awaited trial were hard times for their wives, Doris and Kate, who both had young families to cope with. And it was a sad New Year at Carrants View, too, as Jack and Bessie Bradfield tried hard to keep up the spirits of their two daughters.

The Asum and Wood Norton folk were kind to the children. The Rev Chafey comforted them and spent many hours with Jack and Bessie.

It seems that Tom the Ferret, young Lovely's father, was not pitied in the same way. People reckoned he was partly to blame for the violence in his son.

II

WORCESTER ASSIZES

II

Worcester Assizes

THE CASE CAME FOR TRIAL AT WORCESTER ASSIZES IN March 1890, before Justice Hawkins who said that the accused who stood before him and the Grand Jury were charged with the most serious crime on the calendar. One could not imagine one more serious.

The events of the night of November 10th were repeated. Counsel for the prosecution asked for a statement made by the deceased gamekeeper to be read before the jury.

Thomas Cox, clerk to the Petty Sessions, said that he had visited Stephens' house at five p.m. on November 16th, when Stephens identified Joseph Boswell. Stephens' statement had told the Asum bench how, armed with an ordinary stick, he saw three men approach along a little ride. First he thought they were keepers, but at thirty yards under the bright moon he could see each man had a hat and two dogs and bags for taking game.

"I swear Joe Boswell was one. He had a soft felt hat on and a dark jacket. The other man was taller. The other short. I know Joe, for three years ago I worked on the land with him for two months, scuitching. The dogs were loose, they jumped on me, but none of the men hied them on. The bags were guano bags."

It was his duty, the statement continued, to go and see them. Joseph Boswell started to pelt him with stones from his pocket. Then, when the stones were exhausted, Joseph Boswell struck him a blow with his fist. Then one of the three, who he thought was Joseph, tried to throttle him. Stephens then said he bit Joe Boswell's finger and he fell to the ground, where the other two men kicked his head and body. He became unconscious for a minute or two. When he regained consciousness he found his way to Benjamin Wasley's house.

Keeper Wasley repeated how he had harnessed his pony into the cart and driven Stephens to Dr Haynes at Asum who treated him for several days, including the operation described at the Petty Sessions.

The question was who were the keeper's assailants? Stephens recognised Joe Boswell before he lapsed into a coma, but he could not identify Samuel Boswell, and Lovely Hill.

Counsel for the prosecution described how the prisoners lived in Asum and on November 9th were in a beer house known as the Jolly Gardeners with James Boswell, another brother, and Thomas Spragg, a labourer of Bewdley Street. Alfred Hill came late, about ten o'clock. Thomas Spragg repeated the damning words he claimed to have heard—"Let the buggers come and we ull knock thur bloody yuds off." And Fanny Moyle the barmaid maintained she had been too busy to hear what was being said.

"Do you have a good business there?" asked Mr Amphlet for the Crown.

"Yes."

"A hundred customers that night?"

"No, nor fifty."

The judge remarked that business was good if there were fifty.

"Twenty," Fanny Moyle stated.

Mr Amphlet asked if Tom Spragg stayed until closing time. Fanny Moyle replied she didn't know.

Samuel Boswell denied he was in the woods that night, and repeated that he was out with a man named Hirons. He pleaded Not Guilty.

The Clerk addressed Joseph Boswell: "Do you plead Guilty or Not Guilty?"

"Not Guilty of murder, Sir. I admit I was in the woods, but Not Guilty."

The Clerk to Alfred Hill: "Do you plead Guilty or Not Guilty?"

"Not Guilty, Sir."

The Judge enquired if the men required learned counsel and appointed Mr Cranstoun, Q.C.

Mr Amphlet for the Crown referred next to the operation done by Dr Haynes. The operation was professionally carried out, he stated, and Stephens' eventual death was due not to this but to a murderous blow.

Mary Johnson of Haynes Place, Asum, said she saw Joseph Boswell at ten twenty p.m. on November 9th. By his side was a young dog.

The Judge: "The colour is more important than his age."

Mary Johnson: "It was a brown dog."

The Judge: "Did he visit his brother and cross Littleworth Street?"

Mary: "Yes, he did."

Mary Ann Smith, a single women of Littleworth Street, then described how she lived opposite Joseph Boswell and knew the family well. She said that Sam and Joe Boswell had moved to that street from Ayshton, and lodged with the elderly Bradfields. On the night of the November 9th she went to Joseph's house and heard children crying. The door was shut, a lighted lamp was on the table and as it was eleven fifteen she was worried.

"I had undressed," she said, "but slipped a few things on to cross the road." Fetching the baby downstairs, she nursed it until it stopped crying. While she was in the kitchen Mrs Boswell's brother, Phil Bradfield, came in. She asked him about Mrs Boswell and talked for a quarter of an hour. He went away and came back with a man named Vicarage.

"I then went to Mrs Boswell's mother's house, old Mrs Bradfield, at nigh on twelve o'clock and met Mrs Joseph Boswell coming down Brick Kiln Street. It was quarter past twelve, long after bedtime, so I left the family and went home."

The Judge asked her whether Joseph Boswell was at home.

Mary Smith replied, "No, my Lord, for certain."

P.C. Brinton then described his visit to Joseph Boswell's house at four ten a.m. on November 10th. A brown lurcher lay in front of the fire.

Joseph Boswell interrupted.

"I want to tell you something. Wait a bit." And turning to his brother Sam he said, "I've told them about thee and me and Alf."

The Judge: "Who is Alf?"

Joseph Boswell: "Alfred Hill—Lovely Hill."

Joe Beard was called, a labourer who lived near Joe Boswell. He described the morning of November 10th at four a.m. as being light as day with a full moon. He said he saw Joseph Boswell go first to his rabbit hutch then to the closet. P.C. Brinton and Sergeant Turner were in the street. Beard saw Samuel Boswell come out of his house. "When he saw me he pulled his billycock hat over his left eye, but I recognised him, though."

Elizabeth Boswell, wife of James Boswell of Bewdley Street, said Joe came to their house on November 9th and asked James if he would like a run out poaching. James said no. Joseph said, "Bugger ya."

She saw Joseph again next morning with Lovely Hill. Elizabeth Boswell said, "I told him, 'Well old un, you had has liked to have had it this morning!' "

She said Joseph whispered, "For God's sake don't split a word. We have nigh killed a keeper. When I had his throat he made a cackling noise. Sam kicked him."

Elizabeth Boswell said she saw Lovely on Sunday marked with a scar.

Mr Cranstoun for the defence asked Elizabeth Boswell if Joseph Boswell had been a good friend to her.

Elizabeth Boswell: "No, not exactly."

Joseph Boswell told the court, "I never thought Lovely Hill ud hit the keeper that hard. I said, 'Good God, thee hast killed him.' "

Mr Cranstoun concluded his defence, and addressed the jury. "Surely this is manslaughter in the heat of passion. Men have fought manfully together. The keeper admitted using his stick and had he shown forbearance and not arrogance the crime would not have happened. It is a sudden quarrel, no more. This was not premeditated, regardless of the doubtful evidence of what Spragg said he heard in the Jolly Gardeners."

The Judge in his summing up said that if three men go out to burgle on land where game is preserved and kill a man in pursuance of their crime, they are guilty of murder and no premeditation need be proven.

Under an act of George IV a keeper had a right to arrest men in search of game at night. But if Stephens was thought to have provoked his assailants in the first place the verdict should be manslaughter.

The jury disagreed and went to the locked room the second time. One juror said he wouldn't agree in a month. The Judge said try another twelve hours. The third time the jury returned in ten minutes.

The Clerk: "Are you agreed?"

The Foreman: "We are."

The Clerk: "Joseph Boswell. Do you find him Guilty or Not Guilty?"

The Foreman: "Guilty."

The Clerk: "Samuel Boswell. Do you find him Guilty or Not Guilty?"

The Foreman: "Guilty."

The Clerk: "Alfred Hill. Do you find him Guilty or Not Guilty?"

The Foreman: "Guilty, but a strong recommendation to mercy."

The Judge: "Prisoners at the Bar, you stand convicted. What have you to say why the court should not give you judgment to die according to the law?"

There was complete silence.

The Judge donned the black cap. As he did so he said these words to the men.

"Endeavour during the few hours that remain earnestly to prepare for death. Think as you descend the steps that from within these walls you will never emerge alive. Make your peace with Almighty God who alone can pardon and forgive your great sin. The sentence of the court upon you is that each of you be taken hence from where you came and then by lawful execution that there each of you be hanged by the necks until he is dead. When you are dead your bodies will be buried in the precincts of that prison where you are confined. Before the execution of the dread sentence upon you, may the Lord have mercy on your souls."

Sentence was fixed for March 11th, 1890.

12

NO REPRIEVE

12

No Reprieve

THE HOME SECRETARY TOOK NOTE OF THE JURY'S strong recommendation of mercy for Lovely Hill. Near to the time of execution Hill was reprieved and given a life sentence.

The local paper reported that week how strong the feelings were in Asum, not because of Hill's reprieve, but because the Boswell brothers had not been granted mercy also. The Mayor of Asum was bewildered. He maintained, and rightly so, that Samuel Boswell was the man least concerned in the attack on Fred Stephens. "Why not reprieve all three?" he said.

Two hundred and fifty ladies sent a telegram to Sir William Temple, the Asum M.P. "ALL EQUAL IN GUILT OR EQUAL IN

MERCY". Other telegrams went from Pershore and Birmingham. Fred Cox of Asum appealed to the Prince of Wales. The Vicar, the Rev Correy de Bentley Correy, was no milk and water parson, but a soldier for the right and he telegraphed the Home Secretary: "UNIVERSAL INDIGNATION BY THE WHOLE COMMUNITY OF EVESHAM THAT A REPRIEVE IS NOT EXTENDED TO THE BOSWELLS. PRAY DO ALL YOU CAN. I WILL SEE YOU AT THE HOUSE TONIGHT"

The Rev Correy de Bentley Correy left Asum Station by the seven thirty p.m. Great Western train to see the Home Secretary in London.

I wonder whether a Vicar of Asum before or since has ever gone to such lengths of compassion for men who were of his flock but never his fold. He must have had mixed feelings, but he knew that the folk of Asum were behind him. At midnight at Westminster the Asum priest met not the Home Secretary—he was on other business—but his deputy. Until morning broke the Rev Correy de Bentley Correy wrestled with words on the Boswells' behalf. He tried but failed to convince the Home Secretary's department that the Boswells should be reprieved. The Vicar returned on the morning train a tired and disillusioned man.

It was now a foregone conclusion that the Boswells would be hanged on the Monday.

On Saturday a large party of relations and friends went by train to see the men for the last time, they included Mrs Sam Boswell and her five children, Mary Ann Driver, Mrs Joseph Boswell, William Proctor, and Mrs Quinton. The spectacle of such a party weeping through the streets of Worcester to the Castle Street gaol caused a stir in the city.

At the gaol Samuel Boswell kissed his wife fondly. His children were held up in turn to kiss their Dad between the prison bars.

Samuel said with much emotion that he hoped the children would not want. His wife replied that Samuel had always been a good husband to her. She said she would work in the fields and earn one shilling and three pence per day, but would have to pay someone sixpence to look after her children and her rent was two shillings and eightpence per week.

Lovely Hill who had been reprieved was very cut up about the whole affair and felt badly about the imminent hanging of the Boswells.

"The boys were never born to die at the rope end," he said. After the parting in Castle Street gaol, Mr Cookson entertained Lovely Hill's family to refreshments at the Berkley Arms. The Boswells' family and friends went to Cook's Coffee House.

13

THE EXECUTIONS

13

The Executions

AT SEVEN THIRTY A.M. ON THE MONDAY MORNING journalists marched at the head of the gaoler at Worcester Prison into a small building like a barn or coach house. Here they stopped and saw a glaring bright whitewashed room with a wooden floor.

The hangman and his assistant stood beneath a beam twelve to fifteen feet high, crossing from wall to wall. They were giving final preparation to their handiwork—the apparatus of death. On the beam there were three iron clamps with loops; from two of these loops hung ropes. One loop was vacant, speaking of Lovely Hill's reprieve.

Over one rope was written "Samuel Boswell: 150 pounds". Over the other, "Joseph Boswell: 140 pounds". It was decided by the hangman that Samuel Boswell was to do a five foot eight inches drop, Joseph Boswell was to do a five foot six inches drop.

The ropes were clean and new.

Berry the hangman talked to his assistant. The reporters were asked to stand back. The pit was ten feet deep. Berry measured it, seven feet eight inches wide.

The Boswells were brought in, Sam wearing the same slop or smock coat as he had been arrested in. The voice of the prison chaplain began chanting the burial service. Behind him were the Governor and other officials to witness the execution.

As Berry pinioned Samuel Boswell with leather belts, his assistant pinioned Joseph. The two men had white caps over their faces. Samuel had collapsed as he entered from the condemned cell, his body paralysed for a second or two.

As Berry strapped Samuel's feet the prison clock stood at one minute to eight. Their necks were noosed.

Joseph said, "God have mercy."

Sam uttered, "Christ have mercy."

Standing on the scaffold Joe called out, "Oh my poor wife!"

Sam said, "Ah, my wife and children."

Joe turned to Sam said, "Goodbye Sam."

Sam replied, "Goodbye. God bless you, Joe bwoy." Sam moaned again.

The prison clock struck the first stroke of eight. The trap doors parted. The men went together to the pit with a thud.

Up until twenty-five years before executions had taken place in Worcester in public. My Grandmother told me of these sordid gatherings of folk eager to see the condemned man do what was known as the high jump. That morning in 1890, 1,200 people were in Castle Street outside Worcester Gaol.

"Poor souls," some said. The women were in tears sobbing, "I hope they are happy. They have had their last march."

In Asum it was like a day of mourning. My friend Harvey who died last year described to me the feeling on the land among the workers. Harvey was driving a three horse team at plough not

Asum waits to greet the illustrious guests for the royal wedding.

The tin tabernacle in Asum where the royal wedding was solemnised.

The Duc d'Orleans with his sister, the Princess Louise, and some of her wedding guests at a shoot.

The bag at the end of the royal shoot.

far from Lenchwick. There were four teams working in the same field. Harvey was one of the four ploughboys who worked with four ploughmen. On the March headland where the hedges were bare and the trees leafless in the wind one old carter took out his great turnip watch.

"Whoa chaps, just a minute," he called to his mates on the headland. "Tis two minutes to eight. They ull be hanging the Boswell bwoys directly."

The old carter took off his hat and four men and four boys stood silently until the church clock struck eight o'clock.

Harvey said, "The tears ran down the old man's cheeks and we bwoys felt the same. Not a dry eye amongst us. I'll never forget it."

Lovely Hill did about ten years of his life sentence and became a highly respected market gardener. He died, a gentle old man, almost a lifetime ago. My mother was a lifelong friend of Fred Stephen's widow.

Worcester Gaol is now a garage. The condemned cell is where one of the ramps services cars. Cars are dropped much more gently than the men that Mr Berry hanged there.

14

NEW DUKES FOR OLD

14

New Dukes for Old

1879 WAS A YEAR WHICH GAVE THE PEOPLE OF ASUM AND Lenchwick a new and fruitful topic of speculation in the Whistling Ploughman and the Jolly Gardeners and every fireside in the Vale. For that was the year the old Duc d'Aumale died. Asum got used to having the fourth son of King Louis-Philippe of France living just down the Worcester road on and off for the past fifty years. Now the estate at Wood Norton was inherited by the old Duke's great nephew, the Duc d'Orleans, who was a great traveller.

He and the Duchess lived in grand style and Asum was agog. The one-time country house of an English gentleman was being extended, refurbished and turned into the last word in nineteenth-century extravagance. The Duchesse d'Orleans had very definite ideas about decoration. There were to be fleur de lys motifs over every window and door, and there was word of a marble bath with steps down into it. My Dad was employed by an Asum builder to carry bricks and mortar to the house.

When the Duke returned from one of his Arctic expeditions, polar bears were brought in trucks to Asum station and a bear pit was built. Kangaroos roamed the blackberry bushes. Grandfather Westwood, going fishing at night between the Black Bridges and Chadbury Lock, caught tench and pike and often under the moon saw the wild giraffes looking at him over the high wire fence near the river. Kings and queens, abdicated and ruling, came for the shooting. "All the yud men in Europe," as Jack Bradfield said.

All this social activity at Wood Norton was excellent business for the shopkeepers of Asum. Lowe's—"Our dress mantle making and millinery department is second to none"—had advertised themselves as "Drapers to His Royal Highness, the Duc d'Aumale", and now they had a new plaque over the door, "By appointment to the Duke of Orleans".

My mother worked there as a girl with her needle and thread making ball gowns and riding habits for the royal household, along with Miss Gardener and Miss White. They worked long hours on good honest cloth, shaping and putting together riding habits, for the side-saddle ladies of Wood Norton.

The numerous fittings of that age, the perfection expected in pleasing the Duchess, were an experience she never forgot. How often, I wonder, when the delicate garments had been finished and packed for Wood Norton Hall, did she and her friends in their late teens envy the ladies of wealth and figure and position.

When Singer sewing machines—"made to last a lifetime"—were advertised at less than three pounds on a walnut base, this was still beyond the reach of many Asum women, but how the handles turned and the needles flew up and down like pistons at Lowe's is easy to imagine.

Did the Duchess wear the figure-forming undergarment advertised by Mr Hewlett in Bridge Street? The Platinum Ant-corset which fitted you like a glove, and looked like a coat of armour? I doubt it, for Mr Hewlett was not By Appointment to the French royal family.

The Asum Carriage Factory owned by Coulters in Market Place was. It was patronised by the Duc d'Aumale, Lord Sudeley, Vicount Lifford, Lord Elcho, and—a nice distinction—the Clergy *and* Gentry of the neighbourhood. One hears of bespoke bootmakers who specialise in footwear for hunting and shooting. Well, Arthur Wheatley of Asum went one better and described himself as an Anatomical Bootmaker, and his plaque still stands today. "Bootmaker by Appointment to the Duke of Orleans".

Neighbour Wasley, the Duke's head keeper, rode into Asum town every day and shopped a few odds and ends for the family. He rode the horse with two panniers across its back to carry grocery, in fact anything ordered by the house.

It happened one day the Duke decided to ride to Asum himself. At the Jolly Gardeners after crossing the Black Bridges the horse stopped and refused to budge. Out came the landlord promptly with a lump of sugar for the horse and a pint of ale, expecting to see Neighbour Wasley who always stopped there to whet his whistle. Taken by surprise he gave the pint to his royal guest.

Although the new Duke was popular in Asum and was a good landlord he fell out with Queen Victoria over the Boer War. The Duke made it clear that he did not agree with our troops fighting the Dutch settlers. In fact he was known in royal and political circles as a pro-Boer.

Of course it didn't pay for the ordinary man to be a pro-Boer in Asum. A certain chemist stated his views in public against the War and on the following Saturday, when the town was full of shoppers, several businessmen paid a barrel organ man to play "Soldiers of the Queen" outside his shop all day long. I fancy the chemist was then by Appointment to no one for a while.

Reg Bradfield, Jack and Bessie's son, volunteered for the Medical Corps towards the end of the campaign. An upright market gardener of six feet two inches and every one of those inches a soldier.

Reg was a bright lad, he always had been a quick learner in the art of medicine of the day. He trained at Fort William, under the shadow of Ben Nevis. His trips home to Asum were memorable when this khaki-clad son of the Vale travelled across Scotland and down the east coast by tramp steamer to Harwich and then by train to Asum.

Reg like many of his fellows in the R.A.M.C. was as sick as a dog all the way. A Scottish fish wife cured that after his first trip. "Eat some salted fish, laddie, salted herrings. Ye ull never fall sick then, boy." Reg and his mates took her advice. They stoked up their stomachs with bloaters or kippers before embarking *and* ate them on the journey south. It worked. They were never sick again, and one wonders why.

Sooner than he expected Reg was made Sergeant Bradfield R.A.M.C. and was on his way to the Cape. The British Army now dressed in khaki as a camouflage. Reg said that khaki was an Indian word for dust, and matched the colour of the veld and the mountains.

Typhoid was rampant among the troops who were dying like flies on a winter window sill, and Reg worked closely with the doctors in the field hospital. As a result he learnt a remarkable amount of Latin. He wrote Latin, he thought in Latin. For the medical men wrote down the prescriptions for drugs in that unspoken language. When he got home Reg bought himself books and learnt the Latin names of every flower of the field and hedgerow. However there were drawbacks to that learning absorbed not at University but on the battlefields of Africa. When Reg was ill he knew only too well what the doctor wrote on his medical certificate and later, when his heart became dodgy, he told the doctors in the plainest of Asum speech that he was worn out and no further use.

Reg Bradfield returned from the Boer War and the R.A.M.C. a self-educated man who used his knowledge to advantage. He grew asparagus and fine strawberries on the clay land beyond the black soil of Asum. Reg developed a special strain of wallflowers. Gillies they were called in Asum. With an eye like a hawk he spotted the early flowering blooms which were left unpicked. Putting a nut stick to the individual plant and selecting year by year for seed, Reg developed a wallflower which in a reasonable winter bloomed in February, beating the other little man of the Vale by a fortnight, as his horse and cart took the first pot hampers to market.

One smiles, but admires the sheer spirit of these early gardeners who prized their individual strains of seeds, kept secrets and would never sell or give seed to neighbours.

Reg told me of one hopeful neighbour who came in trying to buy some gilly seed. It's locked in the hovel, he was told, and I'm just off to bed. Good night.

A much more flamboyant contemporary of Reg Bradfield's who also went off to the Boer War was Barlow Cole. Barlow was a hunting man who sailed with a troop of Yeomanry from Southampton. The terrain was unsuitable for Yeomanry or maybe it was Barlow's troop that was unsuitable. The outcome was that when they landed at the Cape their horses were taken unsaddled and used for either artillery or cavalry.

Barlow lived many years in Asum after the Boer War and was a frequent source of amusement for the town. He was a little man, but self-important, who could be seen going to the Worcester races with a waxed moustache and field glasses round his neck, dressed immaculate in bookmaker's check. My mother knew him as Barlow Cole, self-styled American millionaire. This was because he once met a lady of great standing in London and chatted her up, saying that half Asum belonged to him. She fell for his smooth talk and his country tweeds and agreed to come to Asum and marry him. So she arrived at the Great Western Station off the London train, but the first person she met was Barlow, this so-called American millionaire, riding on a muck cart, working for a merchant in the town. It was no good. She recognised him in his cords and his hobnailed boots, his working cap and labourer's neck cloth and took the next train back to the big city.

Barlow Cole, you gather, was a man of so many parts, deceptive to all but the natives of Asum.

15

A RIGHT ROYAL RIOT

15

A Right Royal Riot

THE NEW CENTURY BEGAN WITH THE GREATEST FLOOD ever recorded at Asum, in 1901. It was much worse than the one Charles and Emma Woolen had suffered through when they lived along the waterside. The Northwick Hotel, which was supposed to have been built above the flood level, has a mark on its wall, near the front door, to show how high the water came. That January of 1901 an easterly wind was blowing as the rain teemed down for hours. The floodwater swirled along Port Street and met the flood from the Workman Bridge. Hundreds of sheep were drowned in the river meadows as the Avon rose rapidly. Men stood that day and saw the dead sheep come over the

Workman Gardens and float, like bloated sharks, along the Waterside. John Cox of Oat Street lost two fat pigs which were washed up down Coopers Lane.

An old lady was ill, very ill indeed, and in need of a doctor in her little cottage along Castle Street. The water was deep and the current strong, but Dr Gilpin who lived in that large white house which stands by the drinking fountain, mounted his horse which swam past the corner of Port Street and along Castle Street where he attended to his patient. An act of this kind is remembered a long time in a small town like Asum.

1901 also saw the death of the old Queen. But the people of Asum didn't make too good a start at being Edwardians.

The Coronation of King Edward VII and Queen Alexandra was to take place at the end of June 1902. In Asum the Town Council formed a committee under the Mayor, Bodger Hughes, landlord of the Trumpet Inn on the Green. Three hundred pounds had been raised. The beef and ham feast in the Workman Gardens and the children's tea were to be the highlight of the day under bunting festooned streets.

The King was struck down with appendicitis, then called inflammation, a killer disease when the operation involved was still in the experimental stage. The King's appendix was removed as a last resort and, as we all know, he recovered. At the time the country was shocked and concerned. The Asum folk were concerned, too, but concerned in a different way. Three hundred pounds was in the hands of Bodger Hughes and his committee.

When the first meeting was held in the Council Chamber it was decided, by a majority, that it would be improper to celebrate by feasting and drinking while the King's life was still at risk after the operation. The decision was received with disfavour by a section of the people of Asum. Why should we go without our one day off work, fill our bellies and enjoy ourselves? This won't affect the King's recovery, was the logic of the stubborn smallholders of Asum.

"We beunt a gwain to abandon the festivities, nor the youngsters' tay for Bodger Hughes and his cronies. What about the three hundred quid?" they said.

A second meeting was held by the committee, a proposal being made by Mr Hamilton that the dinner should be abandoned, but the children should have their tea. The Vicar said, however, that surely this was wrong and everyone should go to church and pray for the King's recovery. "We are not going to quibble over three hundred pounds," he added.

Again it was a majority decision to abandon all festivities. Only Fred Hale and Mr Haines supported Mr Hamilton to hold the children's tea.

Bodger Hughes was one of the finest Mayors the borough had ever had. He had sympathy with the town poor and gave five pounds each Christmas to the poor fund of Asum. His little pub on the Green was orderly. Afraid of no one and closing on time, every night, he was the perfect landlord. I'm sure he was guided by what he learnt at his church. For doesn't it say in the Bible "The fear of man addeth a snare." Bodger was not to be trapped in a snare. It seemed a pity he had to bear the brunt of the abuse by the unreasonable section of the town.

As the decorations were pulled down and the shopkeepers agreed to keep their shops open on what was to be Coronation Day, the ugly mob was invited to a public meeting in the market place. The Town Crier with his bell called for everyone to attend. It was a protest against Bodger Hughes and his committee decision.

That evening at seven o'clock Mr New, acting on Bodger's behalf, tried his utmost to speak from the balcony of the Town Hall overlooking the market place, to be answered by boos and catcalls and shouts of "Where's Bodger?"

Mr New suggested that they should adjourn to the Town Hall and no children should be admitted. The children were there in force. This was fun for the young Bradfields, the Sims and their friends who had followed the river path to the market town, especially to listen to grown men and women agree and fall out with each other, just like they did at school.

The angry mob surged towards the Town Hall, but no one could find the key. Mr New couldn't find it and the police were not strong enough in number to prevent ugly scenes in Asum market place.

"We ull force the door down, you," threatened Jingler Jones, a shady market gardener who had boasted that he'd made a thousand pounds out of his well on his holding. He did this by soaking all his market pot hampers until they weighed fifteen pounds, seven pounds over the market's recognised empty weight.

"What be us to use?" Smocky Roberts shouted. "That damn great larch pole with the Union Jack up a top?" Smocky was a little man with chapped hands from the brickyard. Uneducated and gaumless they called him in the town.

Jingler and a few of his mates pulled the pole down across the market place.

"Now my bwoys," he said. "Use it like a battering ram our ancestors used to break through a wall. Give um——"

Give him——

"Lloyd George!" the crowd called out. "Give um Lloyd George!"

Thump, thump, thump, the pole shook the great oak door of the Town Hall. Just in time, before any more damage was done and the mob grappled with the police, Mr New arrived with the Town Hall key. With difficulty he opened the door and a confused mass of people rushed through, hustling the police who just managed to drag the children out. Four hundred of the mob mounted the stone stairway to a room above what was a market hall and the door was closed. The shouts of the folk outside could be heard all over Asum and as far as Donnybrook.

Mr New attempted to take the chair and appealed for order, emphasising that the King's health was more important than the jollifications that Asum had looked forward to.

"Chuck Bodger out," the men shouted.

"What about the provisions?" a voice called out.

"Oi, bury um."

Another voice said, "Send um back to the butchers."

Mr Hamilton said it looked as if the majority wanted the dinner so they should have it and use the food. The hear hears echoed from the hall.

Then a shout from Smocky Roberts rang through the Town

The author's father and mother

Uncle Fred.

A tabber and tut band.

The Pinvin Sports committee, 1912. The butcher from Drakes Broughton turns the spit.

Hall, "Oi, but what about the tay?", meaning the children's tea.

Mr Hale and Mr Haines proposed and seconded that the dinner should proceed, cheered by the crowd.

The chairman explained that this was impossible as it had been cancelled by the Council.

"Who?" Jingler shouted. "Bodger? Then drown him in the river!"

Mr New could no longer be heard as chairman.

The meeting ended in uproar.

Next day Jingler Jones and Smocky Roberts got a coffin from a local undertaker and, painting it black, wrote Bodger Hughes' name on the lid. The mob who had not worked that week, but sat in the morning drinking plum jerkum or cider from brandy casks were beside themselves with anger. The coffin was carried shoulder high up the main street and placed outside the Trumpet where Bodger was landlord. The police had been guarding his house day and night, as one and another tried to set fire to it. Then the black coffin was burnt on the Green, after being burst open and an effigy of Bodger Hughes burnt with it.

After these ugly scenes in June, the Coronation went off peaceably enough when it eventually took place two months later. In the Vale and on the hills around, Coronation night was observed by the lighting of bonfires. The Rev Harcourt Fowler organised a party of fifty men from Elmley Castle, carrying lighted torches to the top of Bredon Hill, and arranged with Overbury, Bredon, Kemerton, Ashton-under-Hill and Beckford to form a pattern of fire like a fiery snake, as torch bearers made their way up from all sides of the outcrop of the Cotswolds.

They made their way to the top where Parson's Folly stands, a thousand feet above sea level, where a fire of gorse awaited the lighting. It was intended, and this was a scheme worked out by the Rev Fowler, that the torchlight procession would be seen from the Vale forming the letters E and A, for King Edward and Queen Alexandra. But someone mistimed the ascent which was made in heavy rain, so the pattern never really took shape.

On Bredon summit a rocket fired from Malvern was a signal for the fire to be lit, and up went the Bredon Hill gorse. The

Malverns have always been a beacon site. Remember Macaulay on the Armada, "Till twelve fair counties saw the blaze on Malvern's lonely height."

As two hundred men stood on Bredon that night the Kemerton Drum and Fife band played suitable tunes. These bands were known locally as tabber and tut bands. As the men looked across the Cotswold, there was a blaze on Cleeve Hill and nearby Dumbleton. Then Dover's Hill above Chipping Campden, famous for Robert Dover and his Cotswold Olympics, lit up, and nearby Ilmington Downs, Edge Hill famous for its battle, Meon Hill above Stratford-upon-Avon, and so on away towards the industrial Midlands, and the Ridgway.

These Coronation fires on the Cotswolds could be seen from as far away as the Radnor Forest, the Black Mountains of Brecon-shire, the Sugar Loaf, near Abergavenny, the Forest of Dean, and the Wrekin.

16

GOLDEN GATES, TIN TABERNACLE

16

Golden Gates, Tin Tabernacle

The Coronation was over but at Wood Norton Asum had its own continuing local pageant of royal comings and going—crown princes and crown princesses, dukes and duchesses. One French duchess broke her leg hunting the Bredon Hill fox, and had it set in plaster of Paris by an Asum doctor who went on to be a famous Worcestershire surgeon.

Then the Duc d'Orleans invited his elder sister and her husband to stay. This was the King and Queen of Portugal. The King was a great shot and a thousand pheasants were bagged in one day during his stay at Wood Norton.

That was the year Reg Bradfield took his wife, Alice, to a little lodge on the estate and became an under keeper.

"Oi, and our Reg did see summat on that big shoot as takes some swallowing," old Jack Bradfield told the beer drinkers in the Jolly Gardeners. "The Duke, I suppose, bet the King that he couldn't have two pheasants falling in the air at the same time from his gun and, damn me, if he didn't have three all dropping together."

"Quick loading by the loader as loads the two cartridges into his second gun," replied his third son, Phil, knowingly. "Twas Keeper Wasley, I warn."

Jack Bradfield was not happy about the state of affairs at Wood Norton. Everything was sacrificed to sport. Great heaps of wood faggots were left for years to harbour the rabbits which burrowed shallowly beneath them. Then, when the faggots were removed by the men, the rabbits bolted, "As thick as fleas on a hedgehog's back," Jack said. "Eight of the gentry shot 3,276 rabbits on Bredon slopes last wick. Says here in the paper. Shooting and hunting unt everything when the gates bunt attended to, nor the drainage. Shameful to see good land neglected 'cos the landlord got wild ideas."

Jack Bradfield, who had enjoyed the merriment of two royal Jubilees when Queen Victoria had her Golden and Diamond celebrations, said that he couldn't hobble to Asum to see the nobility of Europe arrive at the Great Western Station.

"In fact," he said, "Ya know, Phil, I used to be able to carry two hundredweight and a quarter of wheat in a sack. Nowadays it's a job to carry the empty sack."

Jack was now part worker for anyone. He looked to his son Phil. It was fifteen years since Fred Stephens had been beaten to death in the woods at Wood Norton near the cross road. Phil was wont to wax philosophical on the subject. "Ah," he would say, "the drink did me a good turn that night. I'd had a drop too much of your liquor from the bee hives and couldn't rise from the rag rug in front of the fire. I'd ave bin hung else, along with Sam and Joe."

"Potent drink metheglin is," his father said.

Soon there were to be even greater royal excitements than the crack shot King of Portugal. It began with the golden gates. As Jack Bradfield walked one Sunday from nearby Ayshton, he saw two partly completed stone pillars at the foot of the drive to Wood Norton. Neighbour Wasley was also admiring them thoughtfully.

"New gates a gwain yer, Master Wasley?" Jack ventured a question.

"Yes, golden gates the Duke's having put there, decorated to a nicety."

"Golden Gates!" Jack's breath almost left his ageing body. "The only Golden Gates I yeard of is when the Reverend Chafey has spoken of the Gates of Heaven the foew time I've been over to his service. Who's a going to hang these here gates, Master Wasley?"

"He's already come from France, stopping along with Mr Shepherd and his wife up at the Home Farm."

"Nice place the Home Farm. Unt that where the Duke of Edinburgh stayed when Wood Norton house was full of French and Portuguese and Spaniards?"

"Another man is come with him with the gold to put on the gold leaf."

"Oh, they baunt solid then," Caleb said with a certain amount of relief.

Then, in that autumn of 1907, it became known to a breathless Asum that the Princess Louise Françoise, youngest daughter of the late Comte de Paris, and sister of the Duke, was to marry Prince Charles of Bourbon Sicily from Wood Norton. There would be a royal wedding in Asum.

Fanny Moyle, the barmaid, passed the local paper to Neighbour Wasley who read out loud to the knot of customers in the Jolly Gardeners, "Lord Coventry says it's the first royal wedding in Worcestershire for six hundred years."

"Six hundred years. That's a hell of a while ago." Jack Bradfield smacked his lips as they closed on his pewter pot.

"Yes," Neighbour replied, "not long after the Battle of Asum, 1265. Now that's one date I do remember because it was fought in our woods by the river, but I see that Lord Coventry has asked the gentlemen of Worcestershire to subscribe a maximum of two guineas each towards a wedding present to buy some Worcester china for the royal couple."

Of course, nothing would satisfy the Duke, but he must build a new chapel for the ceremony, and import twenty-five bandsmen to play in it. It was built in a Roman style with a great vaulted roof supported by stone pilasters. Cloisters joined the new chapel to the big house, the stone blocks all carved with the fleur de lys. He also had a marquee erected for the grand reception, painted in an antique style on the canvas. This was in addition to the banqueting hall, eighty feet by forty feet decorated in a Louis XVI style. To crown all the whole of Wood Norton was lit by electric light.

Some little time before the wedding the streets of Asum were festooned in gala fashion, while those who could, met the London trains to see the guests arrive. As the special trains drew in at Asum Station the townsfolk saw the glitter of the fabulous uniform worn by the King of Spain, and the lace, diamonds and pearls which draped his Queen. The Queen of Portugal and the Duc de Guise came in a dining car from Folkestone after their Channel crossing from Boulogne. There were ambassadors from Spain, Russia, Austria, Belgium, Denmark, Norway, Greece, Romania, Serbia, and the United States of America. All these people were met personally by the Duke and Duchess who put fifty cars at the disposal of their guests.

So great were the number of guests it was impossible for all of them to stay at Wood Norton. Some stayed at Bretforton Manor, the home of Squire Ashwin. Others from the great centres of Europe stayed at Croome Court. Miss Randell, who lived in that beautiful house overlooking the bend in the River Avon near Chadbury, took in some guests to stay with her. The Star at Worcester was full of folk speaking in foreign tongues. While the Northwick Hotel that week only catered for the wedding guests.

The ladies spent their time sightseeing around the Vale of Asum, visiting such places as Worcester Cathedral and the Malvern Hills. Up until now everything seemed to be going well for the wedding. The autumn pheasant shoots occurred at Wood

Norton as regularly as Easter at the church or the sheep shearing in June. This year the Duc d'Orleans had seen that his coverts were well stocked with game for the men to have shooting parties. So kings, dukes, ambassadors and emperors shot the gaudy November pheasants which Keeper Wasley had reared and shown so well. The sticks of the beaters rattled against the ash and nut trees, making the birds take wing over the rides to be shot by guns from north, south, east and western Europe.

It's reported that the Contesse de Paris shot a stag with her rifle.

The Duke in his own style opened his museum. It was known that he had only recently returned from the North Pole with polar bears for the bear pits. In the museum itself stuffed tigers and lions were realistically poised. A bit gruesome for anyone with a delicate stomach, as the red liquid flowing from the creatures of the wild which had fallen to the Duke's gun really did look like blood.

So November 16th was but days away, when the Roman Catholic Bishop of Birmingham was to make the royal bride and groom man and wife in the chapel at Wood Norton.

Then came the great problem. It was discovered that the chapel was not registered for marriages. The Registrar could not take his book there. One alternative was left to the Duc d'Orleans. The civil ceremony would have to take place elsewhere, but where else could it be held? A Roman Catholic wedding could not be solemnised at Worcester Cathedral.

In the High Street of Asum plans had been made to build a Roman Catholic church to house the Catholic population of the town, but it was yet to be built. Meanwhile the Catholics worshipped in a tin tabernacle on the site. Built in corrugated iron, painted with lead, these places of worship have been common in Britain for the use of the folk outside the Establishment, who put up uncomplaining with the blistering heat in summer, the perishing cold in winter and the noise of thunderstorms on the corrugated iron.

The Duc d'Orleans tried hard to keep it quiet in Asum about the altered arrangements which were that early, very early, in the morning the Registrar would witness a civil marriage in the tin tabernacle. Few would be invited, just the close relatives of the Prince and Princess. Word however got around the town, so that on that morning High Street was packed with sightseers. One must feel sorry for the Duc d'Orleans for this to happen to him after he had built his elaborate chapel and plastered his gates with gold leaf for this glorious occasion. Have a Prince and Princess ever been married in a corrugated iron hut before, I wonder?

17

THE LITTLE MASTER OF MEN

17

The Little Master of Men

THE FIRST DECADE OF THE TWENTIETH CENTURY WAS the era of the little master men around the Vale of Asum and Pershore. Express goods trains took truck-loads of their cabbages and peas and asparagus to Birmingham and Manchester and London. In those days the railway was the lifeline of the Vale gardeners who depended on their produce being in the markets by early morning. And it always was, except when the fog came down and slowed the express goods as she puffed her way north.

Asum asparagus, or "grass", was famous, if not considered economical by the agricultural theorists. It was grown in small plots by men who worked with hand tools, then packed in bundles of 120 buds, known as the long hundred, and bound with river withies or willow twigs. For years soot had been used on the asparagus beds, especially in parts of the Vale where the land was on the clay side. Now imported Peruvian guano was being recommended as a new fertiliser, or "artificial", as it was known. A sales representative for the manufacturers hit on a really bright idea to promote his product. He persuaded a farmer on Broadway Hill to spread some guano on a hillside pasture overlooking the Vale in large letters spelling FOOLS. This was in February, when the grass was still in the grip of winter. By May the word showed up lush and green on a backcloth of the yellowish turf of the poor hillside, and could be read from Asum Tower. After that everybody rushed to buy guano.

Some asparagus growers who bought a lot of the stuff were invited to luncheon at an expensive London hotel, and of course there on the menu was "Evesham asparagus."

"We'll try that," they all agreed.

The waiter served everything very properly, down to the last detail which was a finger bowl beside every plate.

"What's that for, dos't recon?" one grower asked his neighbour.

"Oi, why dosn't ex the flunkey maon wi the fittle," was the reply.

"What be the bowls for, if you please?" asked the seeker after knowledge.

"To wash the butter off your fingers, sir," the waiter explained loftily.

The growers had a good laugh. "You asks a damn silly question, you get a damn silly answer!"

They didn't think much of Sir Richard Temple either. He was the Tory member of parliament for Asum who almost lost his seat when he came down and spoke in the Town Hall of the folly of men trying to make a living on three acres and a cow. This struck directly at the way of life of his market gardener constituents who worked by hand on their asparagus beds with their special two-tined forks. "Mind them steel forks, Sir Richard. Keep off our steel forks!" the hecklers yelled at the back of the hall. And the walls of Asum town were covered with Liberal posters. Poor Sir Richard knew nothing of the fertile earth which the monks of Asum had tilled before the Reformation, and he certainly didn't know his market gardeners whose motto was "We won't be drove".

In the Vale the little men had a security of tenure on their holdings through what was called "Asum custom". It saved them being beholden to the squire or the big farmers. If a tenant wished to give up his land, he was at liberty to choose his successor and be paid an ingoing payment for the crops already on the land in proportion to the continuing value of the crop. Asparagus beds could last fifteen years, while strawberries only had a five year cycle, but plum trees lasted a lifetime. As the Duc d'Orleans had been impoverished by his sister's wedding and his golden gates, he decided to rent a part of his pheasant cover to a Mr Garret from Pershore.

Mr Garret was a grower of fruit and vegetables and his foreman, Ralph Sims, organised the clearing of the ground and planting of plum trees over about a thirty acre plantation facing south-west, overlooking the Avon. The soil was what is known as fox-earthy—lightish sandy colour. Ralph Sims was a dabster at grafting the stocks of Pershore plums. He grafted them with the now famous Victoria and an early plum Rivers Early Prolific.

Ralph Sims' elder son Jack was a boy of thirteen and left school to work for George Garret. It was a shame that Ralph's health failed just as the trees were planted. He became very ill with pneumonia and only the constant poulticing by his wife, Ethel, saved his life. Ralph's bed was downstairs under a huge open fireplace where he lay with his cane by his bedside to punish young Harry Sims, then a mischievous lad of ten.

Harry still remembers the settle by the fireside where he and Jack could look up inside the chimney and see the birds perching on the top. He remembers the sway and pot hooks where Ethel boiled the great iron kettle and fat bacon in an iron pot, and the spiders' webs criss-crossing the bogey hole by the bread oven. And he remembers helping his Dad to puddle the blue clay into a putty-like substance to hold the raffia-tied plum graft to the stock.

This kept out the drying winds of spring until the stock and graft became firmly united. If Ralph had been well the Sims family would have been cosy under the thatch at Wood Norton.

Mrs Sims was a methodical woman for when the twelve o'clock train steamed out of Asum Station, gathering speed towards Pershore, she slid the vegetable-loaded saucepans along the hobs and hooked the loops of iron on to the pot hooks. Ralph was improving and his dinner was to be ready by one o'clock.

"Pity the privy's so far down the garden under the Pershore plum tree," she said to young Jack. "Tis a burden for me emptying chamber pots from Father."

The privy was by a horse pond at the back of the house, built of wood with a dozen large almanacks, nailed on the inside to keep the wind out. Queen Victoria, Lord Roberts and all the important people of the day graced those walls where inside there was seating for one adult and one child.

Mr George Garret called to see Ralph quite often and brought Mrs Sims a night commode.

"Tis all right, Gaffer," Ralph said, "but I looks forward to sitting in the privy anant the Queen and Lord Roberts."

Many years later when Ralph was in fact dying, he was advised to go into hospital. His son Jack took him and because Ralph was a man who was never parted from his dog, the dog went too. Of course they could not admit the dog, so Jack had no alternative but to drive his old Dad back to his cottage with the dog in the cart. Ralph died a week later, leaving instructions for Jack to shoot his dog the day he was buried.

The small men throve with their plums and cabbages and asparagus but, such is country prejudice, they were always looked down on by bona fide farmers who had sheep and cattle and thought themselves a superior class of men.

Does it all stem, I wonder, from the Book of Genesis, where "Abel was a keeper of sheep, but Cain was a tiller of the ground", and Abel's firstlings of his flock were acceptable to the Lord, but Cain's fruit of the ground was not? "And Cain was very wroth, and his countenance fell." Certainly Will Bostock and

Reuben Cook who were neighbours at No Gains Farm and Taddinton and had been to agricultural college had no time for George Garret. George Garret dabbled as a salesman in Birmingham. He neither hunted, nor shot. He was a Liberal and, what was more, a Baptist, who kept the Sabbath to the letter. At Will and Reuben's farms the cattle had to be fed and the sheep looked after on Sundays as much as any other day of the week. But at the plantation George Garret only allowed young Jack Sims to scare the starlings off the strawberries on a Sunday, which he did by pulling a long string attached to a line of tin cans filled with stones.

Will Bostock could well have planted cabbages on his own black soil, but cabbages were beneath his consideration. Will Bostock farmed No Gains in the way it had always been farmed: thresh some wheat for the rent, sell some cattle for the tythe, sheep's wool pays the shepherd's wage and what is over goes between the farmer and his men. True, he remembered stories of hard times, when the liver fluke killed three quarters of the sheep at No Gains, and many farmers had gone bankrupt. Some had then committed suicide. His father had seen good friends of his pulled out of the Avon, bloated like whales, near Wood Norton lock. But No Gains had survived.

In the inglenook at the farm, Will Bostock and Reuben Cook smoked their long clay pipes and sipped their neighbourly port and remembered their fathers' stories of the good pack of hounds Lord Coventry ran from Broadway which he'd bred from some couples from the South and West Wilts, and the Quorn. It was certainly a different world from George Garret's.

George Garret drove his pony and trap to Pershore fair on June 26th and bought four of the finest shire horses in the Vale, all five-year-olds warranted sound in wind and limb and good workers in all gears—all gears being a common term which means that they would work in the chain trace harness and between the shafts of a cart or waggon as what Shakespeare called a fill horse or filler.

So Captain, Merryman, Prince and Noble arrived at the plantation with coloured ribbons in their manes and tails, clip-clopping four in line each with his brand new halter tied to the tail of the horse in front.

"Now there's a pretty sight," Ralph Sims said to Ethel as they passed his cottage door that evening. "I'll warrant our gaffer a got summat up his sleeve."

He had. He had bought a farm at Drakes Broughton and here he was going to show Reuben and Will that he could farm as well as grow plums and be a salesman in Birmingham market.

The man George Garret put in charge of his shire horses was Ron Bradfield. From what seemed like nowhere Ron Bradfield had appeared at the Garrets' straight from the Boer War. He had arrived quite unexpectedly with other men in uniform at Pershore Station off the London train.

Ron who had worked with the Army horses pulling the guns was now ploughing and planting the plantation for Mr Garret, so he was the obvious man to work Drakes Broughton.

A come-down, Neighbour Wasley had said, for a one-time groom to wear hobnailed boots and follow the sweating farting horses, lumbering in front of the plough. Back at Wood Norton Phil Bradfield, who was now a groom himself, probably thought the same about his brother's return to the land. But it was, after all, in their blood. Old Jack Bradfield had worked a lifetime on the soil, most of it for the Bostocks at No Gains Farm, and now he had become part of the soil he loved in Lenchwick churchyard. He and his wife Bessie had died in the same week and been buried together by the Rev Chafey.

Phil Bradfield had his under grooms and strappers and kept enough hunters to serve the Duke's family. When he had a pair of young hunters to exercise he rode very upright with long stirrups, yeomanry fashion, and the fleur de lys on the horse rugs glittered and shone like the hunters' sleek coats. He rode the Worcester road and at Pinvin talked to old Ralph Sims.

At Drakes Broughton he saw his brother Ron ploughing the stubbles with his four horse team. The land was heavy and George Garret wanted it ploughed deep. The steaming horses, baited each day with ground beans and oats and sweet red clover from a year old rick, were driven by Jack Sims.

Mr Garret's handling of Drakes Broughton made Will Bostock and Reuben Cook take notice, especially when a bunch of Garret's bullocks topped the market at Asum cattle fair.

Though he never forsook his first love, plums, George Garret had now established himself in the Vale. But people have long memories, and Will and Reuben would merely pass the time of day with George Garret in Asum Smithfield market.

As sons of tenants on the Duke's estate and now tenants themselves, Will and Reuben thought themselves superior beings to George Garret, the dissenting Liberal, who dealt in fruit in Birmingham market. Hunt Balls at the Lygon and stirrup cups at Wood Norton when the hounds met were not for the likes of him, even if he did top the market with his cattle at Candlemas Fair in Asum and grow good crops of square heads master wheat on the Drakes Broughton clay.

Picture a man dressed for Sunday chapel in Pershore, a well-built man in a clerical grey suit with gold watch chain across his waistcoat, a carnation in his buttonhole and rosy cheeks from his week in the fields, arriving at the Broad Street Baptist chapel from Drakes Broughton on a cushion-tyred bicycle.

George Garret had married Nanny Boltwright who had been a nursing governess to the children of the Lord Mayor of Birmingham. Before her marriage, while being courted by George in the park around the Abbey, she had been known to the folk of Broad Street as Nanny Boltupright.

At chapel on Sunday mornings when George insisted on arriving on his bicycle, Nanny was driven over from Broughton in the pony trap by Jack Sims. She made her entrance to the front pew with George, looking as if she had come straight out of the Royal Doulton factory, so delicate and exquisite was she in her dress and manner.

What a contrast to fat old Joe Sutch, the Pershore butcher, whose face came closely akin to the colour of the beef he sold and whose shoe size and gait resembled one of the Duke's bulls in the dairy enclosure.

Nanny had this dignity, having travelled a great deal with her employers in Birmingham where she had met the great Radical statesman, Joseph Chamberlain, while his children and the Lord Mayor's had parties together.

George was generous to his chapel and shrewd in the market, with a fat pass book at the bank. I knew George, I've heard him preach. He struck me in his later years as a little bombastic, after he took his seat on the County Council. It was a general election that brought George into the forefront of Worcester politics. His fluent chapel-trained speeches in favour of Liberal government were listened to by all except the top Tory class of the Vale. When the Pinvin folk had to travel to Pershore to vote, George Garret put two ponies and traps at the disposal of the party, beribboned and decked with Liberal colours. Jack and Harry Sims drove the loaded carts with the working men and tradesmen of Pinvin to the school at Pershore to vote.

Jack still remembers those trips and remembers a spectacular accident he witnessed in a great thunderstorm when he crossed the old Worcester road. A carter was ploughing with four horses in line on the plough, driven by a lad with a whip. The brass knobs on the foremost horse's harness stood high above the collar and this attracted the lightning flash and, like a stone the foremost horse fell in the furrow. The electric current travelled along the trace or chain harness from foremost to lash horse, from lash horse to body horse, and they all fell dead in front of the plough. The filler horse attached to the plough beam fell with the rest, as the electric current followed the traces, and the carter holding the plough tails or handles fell dead with his team. Jack said the ploughboy still holding his whip beside the team escaped, but stood as if frozen to the ground dazed at the sight he had seen in a flash.

So Jack remembers that election when the Tory Sir Richard Temple held the seat by only ninety votes. A recount at Asum still put the Tory ahead, but George Garret almost succeeded in helping a Radical to represent his part of Worcestershire at Westminster.

A great man of principle was George; he refused to pay his rates when the Church of England schools were subsidised by the ratepayers. He was summonsed and an order was made to sell his bicycle, but no auctioneer would accept it. He probably paid in the end, but paid under protest.

George with all his Liberal and Baptist fervour was a man to be admired. He was honest and industrious, without being greedy, and he was just plain shrewd in business. But he worshipped Nanny Boltupright. In those days the local brass band played at weekends around the houses of the master men of Pinvin and district. So when Nanny was taken seriously ill, George asked the band not to play outside his house that weekend. They played at Bostock's and Cook's, then, full of parsnip wine as strong as whisky, made by Reuben Cook, the band played "Lead kindly light" to the tune Sandom on George Garret's lawn.

George prosecuted them at Pershore petty sessions and they were fined a nominal fine to teach them a lesson.

Nanny? Oh, she got better and lived for years. The bandmaster told me he thought it was "Lead kindly light" that cured her. I believe it was George's kindness and consideration. He even went to the trouble of putting sawdust down on the road outside to deaden the noise of the farm carts as they passed with their iron-shod wheels. This practice in the Vale of sawdusting the road continued long after George and Nanny's deaths.

When George and Nanny were buried among the Nonconformists in the graveyard, the Vale was poorer, for they had been an example of a different quality of life, a middle way between the hunting and pheasant shooting Bostocks and Cooks and the simple ways of the field and fireside of Ralph Sims.

18

WOODEN PLOUGH AND TIMBER

18

Wooden Plough and Timber

KING EDWARD VII WAS KNOWN AS EDWARD THE Peacemaker. I wonder if he alone was really responsible for the few years when life seemed as calm as a July lily pond, where, apart from the ripples made by the insect-catching swallows, the stillness could almost be felt. Old people say, "That was the time to live my boy. We had hot summers then and real winters." This is basically true, of course, for the first decade of twentieth century in Britain is remembered for those scorching summers and hard winters. Pastures were burnt up while some fields of hay in Asum Vale yielded only three hundredweight per acre. Only the mangolds survived as root crops. Turnips were scorched in the ground. The deep-rooted Sainfoin clover and lucerne were a Godsend on the Cotswolds, providing quite good crops of winter fodder.

Since the deaths of Mr and Mrs George Garret and of Ralph Sims, work on the plum plantations and the Drakes Broughton farm was handled by Jack Sims, while his new master, Oliver Garret, George's nephew from Birmingham, looked after the marketing side of the business.

Ron Bradfield still followed the plough at Broughton, having broken in teams of horses and half a dozen plough boys. Ron had become almost a legendary character in the Vale of Asum, in Persha, as he called Pershore town. He was bent with his age like a willing withypole. It suited his whole make up, for when he ploughed he seemed a part of the implement.

What a cumbersome-looking plough Ron still used! Long and wooden like a canal barge, the shield board made from a pear tree. Why a pear tree you may well ask! It's just because pear wood wears slick or smooth on the Vale clay which does not moot or clog it like it would an iron plough. The newest bread can be cut with a wooden knife, but the doughy crumbs would stick to a steel one.

Garret's carter was at peace with the world in the Vale of his beloved Asum. He thought as Thoreau wrote: "When I paused to lean on my hoe, these sounds and sights I heard and saw anywhere in the row were a part of the inexhaustible entertainment which the country offers."

Ron recognised wealth in tangible things, like his master's land, his houses and stock. He described a newcomer as "not much account, just one horse and a cyart". And he kept his modest stocking of gold safe. For Ron had been careful all his life, never trusting the bank with his savings.

"A smartish stocking Ron has got," Jack Sims used to laugh, as he talked with Oliver Garret from Britain's second city. The hosiers of that day made stockings for sovereigns, narrow and long, the size of the coin itself, so that when we talk of folk having money put by in a stocking they really had something custom built for the purpose.

Capital in banks Ron thought of with suspicion as "only on a bit of paper", and he would tell the story of the Asum bank which was supposed to have gone bust. There was an immediate rush of customers to withdraw their money, but the rumour was stopped by a horse-drawn van unloading wide open sacks, showing golden sovereigns. A clever move by someone, as the sacks were full of wheat with just a layer of sovereigns placed on top for the public to see. This was something Ron Bradfield never forgot. The Bradfields were a careful family, out of debt and out of danger.

At Wood Norton, where a third generation of Bradfields now worked, Neighbour Wasley was getting on. A bit crippled with rheumatism, he still kept a watchful eye on the pheasant coverts and the deer parks, though he had younger men now to rear the pheasant chicks and organise the autumn shoots. Phil Bradfield's son, Jack, named after his grandfather, made a barricade of closely driven stakes at the wood's edge. He covered it with the bracken mowed from the rides, so that the birds, driven by beaters in the narrow paths, or triggs, between the trees, rose high above the waiting guns. Yes, Wasley and his men could still provide a good day's shoot for the Duke and his friends.

Young Jack Bradfield was a little, lissom chap of twenty-two when he was made head forester at Wood Norton. He could swing the seven pound axe and fell a tree like a veteran. The Duke's agent told him to clear a part of the wood where the trees had reached their prime and were fit for the saw mills at Asum. The chips from Jack's razor-sharp axe fell like dinner plates on the green rides of Norton Wood as he notched the butt deeper on the side the tree was to fall. From October until April the ring of axes could be heard along the banks of the Avon, as Jack and his men felled the trees in rows, like men felled in battle on that very spot where Simon de Montfort had bled in a noose-like trap by the riverside.

The sap begins to rise in late February, so the timber felling ceases. Out come the peeling irons to peel oak bark for Asum tannery. Nine tons they sent to help cure the leather, after the bark had been dried for six weeks in sun and wind. Jack supervised the stacking, insisting that large pieces from the oak trunks were piled on top of the stack to shed off the water, a roof, in fact, of oak bark.

The women helped with the faggoting of the brushwood twigs for firewood, tenpence a score bundles tied with wire like boltings of straw.

Nothing was ever wasted. Nut wood went to Redditch to make cotton reels, heatherings were stacked aside for hedge layering. These heatherings are a bit bigger than bean sticks and pliable to finish a well-layered hedge.

The loading of the trees was done by the timber team from Asum— five horses, five men, with the skeleton-looking waggons. To see the timber team, with the horseman standing perhaps ten yards away, and to hear him talk to his horses and tell them when to pull is something to remember. As the traces tighten, the back bands rest high off the horses' slick backs, the faithful beasts go almost on their knees to pull the last ounce, and the tree slides through the bluebelled wood alongside the waggon. Here the most dependable horse is hitched to a rolling chain, while the poles are positioned for the tree to be slid on to the waggon. A pole known as a frightener is placed on the opposite side of the timber carriage as a prop to prevent the tree from upsetting the carriage or going right over. How smoothly those trunks, or sticks as they were known, had to be dressed by the axe so that no knob would hinder the loading.

The felling of timber in Norton Wood left behind a wealth of fencing materials. Young Jack saw that posts and rails were stacked and dried ready to mend the fences and rehang the gates on Bostock's and Cook's farms. The Duke, as landlord, was obliged to provide the timber for these repair jobs.

Daniel Rivers had come to Reuben Cook's farm. He was a master at the craft of layering tall hedges, staking them and binding the top with heatherings until it was impossible for even a rabbit to come through the boundary fence. He had been taught the art by Joseph Arch of Barford, that tireless champion of the farm labourer's rights, who eventually became a member of parliament. Joseph Arch had held meetings around the Asum

Vale villages, but with only a limited support from the labourers. The farmers did increase wages by two shillings a week, but as usual Asum men were an unco-operative lot, independent as independence could be pursued in those days.

Daniel Rivers was a chapel man, walking miles through the Vale villages as a local preacher, like his tutor Joseph Arch, before him in fact. A little Bethel not more than mile from Shakespeare's Avon, tin roofed and timber built, was the setting where a few working men and their wives made music and sang around the harmonium on Sunday nights. Here the half-literate men who had clung to the Gospel stories, unburdened their souls and gave a primitive message in fervent preaching and prayers.

Daniel Rivers stood in his Sunday black among the people who belonged to what was known as the Cause. He thumbed the pages of his well-worn Bible until he came to the book of Daniel.

"Now let's see what Daniel done in his day," he said, before reading from the Book.

Jim Harvey, who worked for Reuben Cook, jumped up out of his seat at the back calling, "Oi, I can tell tha what Daniel a done in his day. He has cut a hedge for Master Cook and took whome the best of the 'ood."

No doubt Daniel had an answer for his friend.

Daniel and Jim occasionally met Harry Sims at the little blacksmith's shop at Lench. Local news and gossip hummed around the forge on wet days when Harry took a horse from Ron Bradfield's team to be shod, while Daniel had his hedge hooks sharpened on the grindstone or new stalcs or handles fitted and perhaps Jim Harvey came for Cook's plough shares.

The forge with its ringing anvil is poetry and art. Its fascination has been sung by Longfellow, made music by Handel and painted by Morland. Is it superfluous to speak of the gleaming red hot iron, the cascade of sparks, the melodious clank of hammers on hot metal? Somehow I don't think so. There's a magic in the blacksmith's shop on a wet dull day. Shadowy light flares through the black cobwebs at the blackened windows, the bellows groan as the smith wields the cow horn handle to woo dull ashes to a flame, coaxing it to life gently, feeding the fire with his little iron shovel. The red hot shoe is fitted to the pan-shaped hoof of the black shire horse of the Midlands or the dainty nimble hooves of the farmer's cob or the Squire's hunter.

There's a smell of burnt hoof and a cloud of yellow fug which the farrier dodges deftly as he makes sure the iron fits the horn of the hoof in a little more than a semi-circle around the soft frog in the middle of the horse's foot.

He drives the nails home through the shoes and clenches them on top of the hoof. Then the man in his leather apron and heavy cord trousers seizes the hoof between his legs and with a rough rasp or file polishes away the edges above the shoe. Then his job is almost over, except for blackening the hooves with a rounded brush like a black lead brush and painting the yellow and brown horny hoof with oil.

Jack Sims spent a lot of time during those hot Edwardian summers in the plum plantations adjoining Wood Norton. He had to supervise the pickers, while Harry Sims took the produce to Asum Station for Oliver Garret to sell in Birmingham market.

The fruit pickers were a nomadic people who tramped the roads between the casual wards of the workhouses in winter, picking the peas and plums of the Vale in summer. Often highly educated but drunken, some were ships' stewards awaiting a boat which never came into port. Others were ruined clerks, most had lost their credentials, all had their stories to tell round the orchard fire where they camped close under the shelter of the hedge. They made rough tents from corn sacks, and fried their bacon over the fire which never went out all the summer, even when the temperature was eighty-five degrees in the shade. Billycans made from toffee or biscuit tins hung from a bent iron stake, cooking their evening meal. Even in the heat of the day many worked in great thick overcoats, on the assumption that what would keep the cold out, would also keep out the heat. Men of wonderful imagination these gentlemen of the road. There was never any disorder in Oliver Garret's plantations, just laughter and song from early morning until sundown.

Jack Sims had more trouble with the local children who joined the pickers. His maxim in the fields, and how true, was that one boy was a boy, two boys were half a boy, and three boys were no boy at all. "The young varments they *ull* play about," he said.

Oliver Garret with his business in Birmingham always paid his Pershore men at the kitchen door on Saturdays. It's odd how the old time farmer always paid his men in the fields, never under a roof. Some rode around on horseback and paid from a leather bag. This gave the farmer a chance to gallop away after the unpleasant sensation of parting with his money. One farmer in the Vale was alleged to pay his men, holding the wages behind him, so that he didn't see the money go into their pockets.

Both Will Bostock and Reuben Cook had bought mowing machines to cut the hay in the riverside meadows. Daniel Rivers was as proud as a peacock as he mowed Reuben Cook's grass in three-foot swathes, with a machine drawn by two horses. But the machines were cutting down on labour, so the Vale folk were grateful to Oliver Garret who employed more men and women on his acreage than the Bostocks and Cooks. He kept them for hand work like hoeing, planting cabbages and picking beans. So the mowing of the meadows at Broughton was still done by a team of men with scythes.

One character on Oliver Garret's payroll was nicknamed Hollow Legs, on account of his capacity for cider. He did odd jobs at the plantation and every Saturday Oliver had to try to run through what he'd done in order to pay him.

"Now what have you done this week?" Oliver asked him one Saturday.

Hollow Legs had been working that week in Oliver's garden while his master had been in Birmingham, and he had been drinking what Ron Bradfield called two man cider. It needed one man to drink it and another to hold him up.

"Well," said Hollow Legs, "I—I—a—planted them thur savelroys. Then yesterday morning I, well I don't like to tell ya, but I cleaned out that thur place, you know Gaffer," and in a whisper Hollow Legs mouthed the word privy, "up the garden, an dug it in the ground, you knows what I myuns. Then I planted the ground with them purple spurters." Purple spurters was Hollow Legs' word for purple sprouting broccoli.

One other thing Oliver Garret did for his workers. He gave them a day off to go on an annual outing to Ilfracombe. Oliver and Maud, his wife, cooked a great joint of beef the day before these outings and Oliver carved while Maud made sandwiches for the men from the black soil who were off to see the sea.

19

A DAY AT THE SEASIDE

19

A Day at the Seaside

My father always remembered the first time he went to Ilfracombe. It was one of those very early mornings in June, when the dew-heavy grass soaked Dad's polished light-weight boots which he called his tea drinkers, that the Asum men met the Ayshton men on the early morning excursion to Sharpness Station.

Uncle Fred, Dad, Job Wheatcroft, Ern Callaway and little Uncle George sat on the red and black moquette seats of the third-class compartment as the trainload of trippers jerked out of Ayshton Station along the Midland Railway Branch line to Ashchurch.

"All change," the ticket collector shouted. "All change for Gloucester, Sharpness and Ilfracombe."

The sun was just peeping over the Cotswold Edge and the cuckoos were competing with the early birds of the orchards of the Vale. Men of the land are accustomed to eat in the early light of dawn, so Uncle George had untied the knots in his red spotted handkerchief as soon as the party had crossed to the main Gloucester train. Uncle's first bite at the fat bacon from a Gloucester Old Spot pig out of Grandad's sty soon had the men's mouths watering. Ern Callaway carried a wicker basket with a peg fastening, the one he used when working as a platelayer on the Barnt Green-Ashchurch branch line.

Uncle Fred winked at Dad and said, "It's all right for some. Ern's got a free pass working for the Company. It's costing us a few shillings."

Some more passengers got on at Cheltenham, "Poor, proud and pretty, they be," Uncle George said to Dad.

Uncle George was a little man, but a great traveller on excursions. Four years older than Dad and still single, he toured the resorts wherever the Midland Railway would take him. "Which way did you come back from Scarborough?" Ern chaffed him. Uncle George should have changed at York, but he was hard of hearing and having a nap and finished up in the Lake District. Uncle took an extra day getting home that trip.

Ern was critical of the track as the coaches rocked across the points below Gloucester. "A feow wedges now and again from the chairs where the lines rest," he said to Job Wheatcroft or Gassy, as he was known, since working at Asum gas works.

At Sharpness the train drew alongside the Severn Estuary. Here the SS *Ravenswood*, a paddle steamer of Cambell's White Funnel fleet, was waiting to take the men having a day for the King, as a holiday was called, down the Bristol Channel. Across the river from Sharpness Docks, Lydney Pier stood out like a partly-built bridge on the high tide.

The little waves lapped the water's edge, against a backcloth of many shades of green afforded by the Forest of Dean's ancient trees. The Lydney shore formed a complete contrast to the south bank where the continuing line of the Cotswold Edge followed the river.

After the *Ravenswood* had completed its first few miles Uncle Fred and Dad and Ern Callaway spotted Thorbury church tower. This reminded Dad of our village doctor's father, the Rev Moncrief Overthrow, who had the neighbouring parish to Thorbury, at Tytherington, and as the *Ravenswood* coasted down the Severn, Dad told the tale of the Rev Moncrief Overthrow and the great duckpond controversy. This was a classic story of a feud between squire and parson in the second half of the nineteenth century. The living was the gift of the Lord of the Manor. The squire decided to make his eldest nephew rector, but as he was still at Oxford he agreed to make Rev Moncrief Overthrow rector until his nephew was ordained. The nephew died at Oxford so the squire wanted to substitute another nephew for the living. "Oh no!" Moncrief said, "that's not the agreement." And he stayed in the rectory, dug his heels in and refused to budge.

The squire then tried to make things unpleasant for Overthrow. He began by knocking down the wall of the Rectory and driving his cattle through the garden. The Rev Overthrow, quite within his rights, locked the door which the squire used as a short cut to the church. The squire smashed the door and drove his cattle through the garden again, then he filled in the village duck pond, enclosed the land and turned it into a garden. The Rev Overthrow sued the squire and won the case. The duckpond was restored and Moncrief Overthrow held the living until his death.

Oddly enough his son, our doctor, who lived at Ayshton, got himself involved in a watery controversy as well. At a vestry meeting he had objected to the village stream being piped down Asum Street. Uncle George wanted to know why. His sister lived in a cottage alongside the stream and had to have a little stone bridge to her front door. Ern Callaway laughed and said it was because the doctor's ducks paddled in the stream.

At that moment Dad and Uncle Fred who sat on deck in the bow of the *Ravenswood* were drenched by a huge wave.

"Dall it if yunt the bore coming up the Channel," said Uncle Fred.

"It yunt, is it?" Joe Wheatcroft asked Ern Callaway who had been further afield at his work than the other men. Some Sundays he did relief work on the line down Bristol way.

As the steamer passed the docks at Avonmouth the suspension bridge over the Bristol Avon came into view for a while.

"There's a masterpiece for you to look at," Uncle Fred said. His father, William, had often talked about the building of that road across the Avon Gorge.

The *Ravenswood* churned the water of the Bristol Channel with her two great paddles. The foam lay, as Gassy said, like a hedgerow of hawthorn blossom in full bloom. Down in the engine room the young men marvelled at the size and thrust of the connecting rods between the steam cylinders. They debated between themselves whether the stokers were black from the coal or men "from away" as they put it. Gassy Wheatcroft soon solved that point because at the gasworks the stokers got black from the coal as they filled the retorts. Compared with the simple brass tackle the men had been used to when following the plough as boys, the polish on the brass in the engine room and the precision of the machinery was an awe-inspiring sight.

At the bar they slaked their thirst with stone ginger beer from stone bottles; nothing stronger for men who had signed the pledge together in 1893.

Although the weather was fair the south-west wind was nippy on deck, as the *Ravenswood* thrashed by the two stranded islands which stood up from the sea between Weston and Cardiff in the tricky tide of the Channel. Flat Holm, the larger one, had a lighthouse and was inhabited, but Steep Holm stood out like a giant lump of rock salt, formidable and grim, the gulls standing sentinel on its clifftop.

"Not a lot of tater ground on that hillock," Ern said.

"When be us going to get to Ilfracombe?" Uncle George asked the barman as he swallowed another glass of ginger beer to swill down his bread and fat bacon.

When he was told they were only about half way, the men went below away from the swell of the sea, marvelling all the time that they were below sea level as the waves lashed against the portholes.

As a G trombone Salvationist Uncle Fred could play most wind instruments, and he had brought with him a little brass cornet he'd bought for ten shillings off a friend in Asum.

"Come on Fred," Dad said. "How about a little tune?" Uncle thought a bit then in the corner of the dining saloon he piped up "Goodbye, my bluebell". The Cheltenham men and women, the Tewkesbury crowd and some of the Asum folk had had their tongues loosened by the good beer of the *Ravenswood* and soon joined in.

"Get the lad a drink," a Tewkesbury farmer called to the barman.

"Stone beer for me," Uncle said. "I'm not breaking the pledge."

"Where do you live? Asum is it?" the farmer guessed. Uncle nodded. "Well come over to my place and drink some liquor worth putting to your lips—Malvern Hill perry. You would play a cornet on that."

Off Minehead the Asum party went on deck as the sea calmed down, and saw the Exmoor ponies grazing in the heather.

"It's a pity the poor craiturs, some on them a whether, be destined to work down the mines," Gassy told Uncle Fred.

After meeting some big ships into Cardiff the *Ravenswood* hugged the Somerset coast, seeing very little of the Welsh side. Then she turned and middled the Channel, so that for the first time they were out of sight of land.

This worried little Uncle George who had previously trusted the railway on his excursions. "Where be us?" he asked Dad. "Think the Captain's lost?"

Uncle Fred winked at Ern and said, "I did hear talk of us going to Ireland. That ull be all right, won't it George?"

"No!" George said, "I got into trouble going to the Lake District the other year. I got to be back to milk Master Taylor's cows tomorrow. Brother Jim is seeing to um today."

The cliffs of Lynmouth were sighted and at Lynton the folk who wanted to get off were hoisted into a rowing boat which came alongside.

"I bunt that ventersome," Uncle George said to Dad. "It's a

hit or miss sort of job. You got to jump in the boat when its anant the steamer.''

The pier at Ilfracombe was sighted by Gassy Wheatcroft from his seat on top deck, but the waves got higher and the *Ravenswood* pitched and tossed and rolled, her decks washed by the Channel waters.

Uncle George, who so far had been eating and drinking his share, suddenly turned a green colour under the stubble of his chin and either side his jet black moustache. Leaning over the rails little Uncle George heaved with the rocking of the steamer and was sick. Sick as a dog he said, and the pier in sight. Uncle Fred just for fun played ''Rocked in the cradle of the deep''.

It was a comical sight as the five men cautiously walked the planks of that North Devon pier. The rolling of the boat had made them dubious about anything which stood over the Bristol Channel. Uncle Fred, the comic of the party, laughed as Ern Callaway said how glad he would be to be on terra cotta again.

Little Uncle George, now revived from his sea sickness, asked Uncle Fred how he came by the grizzly bearskin cap he was wearing.

''It's the only cap like it in Asum,'' Fred declared, ''and it came from either the North Pole or South Pole.''

Gassy cleared his throat in a doubtful sort of way. ''The Pole?'' he said, ''Not many folk ha bin in them regions and I'm sure thee hasn't. I suppose the next thing we shall hear is that the Salvation Army band plays around the Pole and Fred plays the ump ump ump on his G Trombone. Pull the tother leg, ull ya.'' But Gassy was keen to hear the real truth, so Uncle Fred explained how the Duc d'Orleans had been a great explorer who'd spent a lot of time in the Polar regions and filled the bear pits at Wood Norton with creatures brought back from his travels. When one of these ''gristley'' bears died the Duke had its skin made into rugs.

''That dosn't explain where you got that comical hat from,'' Uncle George butted in.

It so happened, Uncle Fred went on, that Mr Samson the Duke's valet who lived in Bengeworth, employed Uncle Fred's eldest, Emily, as nursemaid and it was Mr Samson who gave Emily the hat for Uncle Fred.

As plain as a pike staff, Ern Callaway agreed, but why wear a hat in the summer at the seaside. At this point Gassy Wheatcroft laughed and lifted the peak of *his* cap showing a bald patch, well hidden as a rule. "I allus keeps my hat on when the Gaffer's around as I'm just going a bit bald at the crown of my head and the saying is at work 'Keep your caps on, they are sacking the old uns.'"

"How about dinner?" Ern said, as they walked past the string of restaurants on the hilly pavements of Ilfracombe which from twelve o'clock onwards implored the holidaymakers to step inside. Dad was willing, and my two Uncles and Ern were ready to eat at the first restaurant they came to. But Gassy was different. He wanted value for his money and looked thoughtfully at the bills of fare in all the windows.

"Too dear, Tom, too dear," Gassy said to Dad, shaking his head, and stroking the jet black curl of hair which hung like a pot hook on his brow, in contrast to the bald patch under his cap.

"A good dinner for eightpence," a stout man stripped to his braces called out in the midday sun. He waved a folded newspaper, pointing would be customers to the tables inside.

"Looks cheap," Uncle Fred said, and he, Uncle George, Dad and Ern Callaway walked up to a ready laid table.

"Where's Gassy?" Uncle Fred said looking around. But Gassy was still pondering over the price and he turned away from the door. Taking his last piece of bread and cheese from his pocket he sat on a seat overlooking the sea with his shut knife and ate his midday snack, while his companions started on the eightpenny dinner.

"Roastbeefroastporkboiledmuttonappletartplumtartboiledrice pudding," said the waitress in the white apron.

Uncle George wouldn't have pork because there was no R in the month. He had beef and carrots.

"What vegetables would you other gentlemen like?" the waitress asked.

My two Uncles had cabbage, so did Ern Callaway, but Dad asked for peas. The early peas were just being picked around Asum and nothing tasted quite like the early peas of Asum Vale.

The plates came loaded with the meat and two vegetables. Dad had made a bad choice with his peas. The first one he touched with his fork shot across the room. They were grey and as hard as bullets. He left the peas. Ern Callaway had finished his pork and potatoes and cabbage, but was left with a depth of gravy on his plate. Without a word he clasped his plate in both hands and, tipping it to his mouth, noisily drank the gravy.

"You can't do that here," said Uncle George the much travelled excursionist, who it's to be remembered came home from Scarborough via the Lake District. "They ull throw us out."

"Don't like to see good gravy wasted," Ern answered. "Besides the juice a' got all the goodness in."

Uncle George recommended the rice pudding next, because of his sea sickness on the outward journey. And Uncle Fred paid the two shillings and eightpence after the rice pudding was eaten.

Then they rejoined Gassy on the promenade and all went down into the one little sandy bay. Our young men of the Vale took off their jackets and waistcoats, watched the seagulls, and enjoyed the sunshine and the smell of seaweed. Daring folk emerged from the bathing machines to swim among the waves. These shepherd hut-like contraptions, where the bathers could undress in private and don black cotton combinations to enter the sea, were pulled to the water's edge by ponies.

The ponies pulled them back up the beach as the tide came in and down again as the tide went out.

Uncle Fred fetched more ginger beer from a shop on the sea front. Five bottles he bought, and winking at Dad said, "I reckon we ought to let Gassy have a bottle. That bread and cheese must have been dry. Just think what we had, 'A good dinner for eightpence'."

The *Ravenswood* was waiting at the pier and due to sail at five thirty. "Before we go back," Uncle Fred suggested, "let's buy some fresh fish."

On the quay four young men bought fish at a quarter the Asum price.

"Too dear, Tom," Gassy said. "Too dear."

Back on the steamer the *Ravenswood* barely moved at her

mooring. The Bristol Channel was as calm as a mill pond, the sky was clear and the water blue. A blast or two from the ship's hooter sending a cloud of steam over the quay was a warning to latecomers that the gangplank would soon be up and the journey back to Sharpness would begin.

Picture five men off the Midland clay sitting at the bow of SS *Ravenswood* as she showed them the cliffs of red sandstone, the wood coombs and the little bays of North Devon. They called again at Lynmouth for the few passengers who came out in the rowing boat and be taken on board. The only motion was the back pedalling of the paddles when the Captain brought his vessel to a halt to pick up the passengers.

Then away the party slid softly between the Somerset side of the narrowing Severn estuary and the hills and incomparable beaches of Gower. A happy journey on the water to Sharpness where the Gloucester train waited in the dark of a midsummer night.

Five Vale men had seen the sea.

20

THE END OF UTOPIA

20

The End of Utopia

THE DUC D'ORLEANS LIVED ON AT WOOD NORTON with his Duchess until 1912 and Neighbour Wasley, helped by under keepers, still provided a good show of pheasants for the autumn shoots. But things were not the same on the estate. The deer which dominated the parkland were considered unprofitable by the Duke's agent. The days of the landed gentry who lived their lives in the green fields and woods as if Utopia was theirs and life eternal had begun to disappear like butter in the sun.

The bear pits were closed and the giraffes died. The agent urged the Duke to shoot the deer and sell the venison to London, to fell timber, cut down on the game birds and rent out more growing land for plums. Phil Bradfield's stable was reduced to a mere half dozen hunters, enough for the family and guests at the House to hunt with the Croome. The Duke was sad about losing his old extravagant way of life, but he knew his agent was right. The golden gates and the royal wedding had cost him a fortune, one he had been happy to spend to bolster the esteem of the remnants of the French monarchy. For the same reason memories of the ceremony in the red oxide painted iron tabernacle still rankled. How his pride would have been mollified if he'd lived to know that the grandson of that tabernacle blessed union would one day become King Juan Carlos, the restored King of Spain.

The great shoot of 1912 thinned down the deer to a few stock animals. The Duke himself was a surprisingly talented butcher, and skinned, dressed and packed venison for the London trade in a professional way. Loads were sent by rail from Asum Station. Some even went abroad. The Duchess was no mean markswoman with a rifle. Enjoying the so-called sport with her friends, she shot the young bucks and roes like a sniper. Neighbour Wasley was so upset, he retired to his woodland cottage, leaving the two younger keepers in charge. More trees were felled that winter under the skilful eye of young Jack Bradfield. Money trickled into a waiting bank, and for a while the French exiles were solvent.

It was good to see the following year old Ron Bradfield ploughing the woodland cleared by Phil's son, while Jack and Harry Sims planted more plum trees for Oliver Garret, who had snapped up the chance to rent that southerly slope overlooking the Avon and Bredon where the late spring frosts would not kill the plum blow, on the Hills of Lenchwick.

No one was thrown out of work by the Duke's retrenchments, but the older men were not replaced. In fact, Oliver Garret with Jack Sims, his manager, employed more men than the Duke as his plum plantation grew. He employed more men than the two farmers, Will Bostock and Reuben Cook with their 600 acres put together.

In those days ploughing between the young trees was considered too delicate a job for horses, and the young boys of the

Vale turned plough horses themselves with clanking foot irons strapped to their hobnailed boots. They drove the Asum two pronged fork into the land, turning over the sods between the growing trees in even rows, throwing back the clay and leaf mould of hundreds of years of forest in furrows across every fifteen foot alleyway, in the only way true Asum market gardeners knew.

Wasteful labour some may say, but the merchants and artisans of the North of England had acquired a taste for the Victoria plum and special plum trains left from Asum Station every night of the season, going as far north as Glasgow. Surely Asum had become a garden town, and Pershore its near neighbour produced some of the finest fruit.

Off the Birmingham train arriving in Asum at seven p.m. stepped a middle-aged man. Square shouldered and upright he walked along the platform, over the footbridge, up the hill into the High Street, where he called for a drink at the Railway Hotel. He was soon recognised as Lovely Hill.

It happened that Ron Bradfield was there that night and, seeing Lovely, bought him a pint of beer. A young keeper off the Estate, a keen hawk of chap, reckoned that chap in the corner with the pipe had got something on his mind.

Ron nodded. "Plenty, my boy, plenty."

Lovely had time to think during his life sentence. I wonder that he came back to Asum, but he did. He rented a smallholding over the river at Donnybrook and could be seen about town, a sombre figure sitting on the front of his loaded dray, behind an old pony.

The years passed in Asum from one Mop Day to the next. The Duc d'Orleans had left the neighbourhood, but stories of "goings on" at Wood Norton were to be good tap room gossip for many a winter night to come. Edward VII was dead and George V was on the throne. The era of Edward the Peacemaker was over and in 1914 Asum men flocked to the recruiting stations to enlist. Oliver Garret's plums went to make jam for Kitchener's army in an Asum factory. Wood Norton became a hospital for wounded soldiers.

But Ron and Phil Bradfield and Lovely Hill remembered when Queen Victoria ruled and a plum was named after her.

WHEN VILLAGE BELLS WERE SILENT

FRED ARCHER

In *When Village Bells Were Silent* Fred Archer remembers what the Second World War was like in rural England.

First of all it meant the War Ag, that terrible right hand of agricultural bureaucracy which made wheat grow in what had been bramble-covered fields, but was less successful in ploughing waterlogged meadows. Then there were the evacuees from the industrial midlands, seeking refuge from the destruction wreaked nightly on Birmingham and Coventry, to which Bredon Hill afforded a macabre grandstand view. The Land Girls arrived, determined to keep up with the local sprout-pickers by day, and adding variety to the restricted night life of the village. Eventually there were the Italian prisoners of war. Joyce came from Sutton Coldfield as a Land Girl and Fred wooed and wed her. The Home Guard was formed and went about its manoeuvres with the sensible reflection: 'We beant worth a bom yer . . . they be hellishly expensive to make.' But a stray bomb did fall, on a flooded wheat field, leaving a blue clay hole 'that ud make some smartish bricks'.

There were stories of the pig clubs and a black market of bacon, and of ten tons of cement spread on a field by mistake, and all the comings and goings in a small Worcestershire village which would never be the same again.

176pp 216mm × 135mm
ISBN 0 86299 429 2 (paper) £4.95

YAP

JAN STEWER

This book contains a collection of humorous tales of Devon village life, told in the tongue of the native. The dialect, however, is never obscure and the meaning is always perfectly simple to follow.

Included among these yarns are the amusing account of Jan Stewer playing golf; of the great singing contest between the villages of Pitt Wollidge and Stoke Arrish; of the strange issue of the fortune telling of Abdul the Prophet and of Silas Wonnacott's only performance as a 'waxworks'.

Jan Stewer's tales of Devon village life are relished by every true Devonian, although they are by no means restricted to folk from that county, but are greatly appreciated by everyone with a taste for simple tales of simple life.

160pp 216mm × 135mm
ISBN 0 86299 431 4 (paper) £4.95

JUST AROUND THE CORNER

HUMPHREY PHELPS
With illustrations by Hugh Moss

Humphrey Phelps farms just over two hundred acres in west Gloucestershire. Both his father and grandfather farmed in the same district. He is married and has three sons.

He says he was not the small boy of his story and never had an Uncle George. However, he assures us he knew people just like the characters in *Just Around the Corner*. Sadly, they are disappearing, victims not so much of the passing years but of so-called 'Progress'.

Just Around the Corner records the sadness and the gaiety, the gravity and the humour of village life at the end of the 1930s as seen through the eyes of a mischievous, observant and essentially human small boy. The story leaves a satisfying and agreeable flavour in the mouth.

160pp 216mm × 135mm
ISBN 0 86299 443 8 (paper) £4.95

UNCLE GEORGE AND COMPANY

HUMPHREY PHELPS

Uncle George is back. That lovable old rogue who surfaced in Humphrey Phelp's previous stories of country and farming life. *Just Across The Fields*, *Just Over Yonder* and *Just Where We Belong*, now has a book all to himself.

Some time before the war Uncle George threatened to finish with baking – although, some say, the way he was running it in those last few years, it had almost finished with him too. He became a full-time smallholder, able to follow his natural bent and indulge in all his favourite pastimes.

A shed stood in the garden covered in honeysuckle and it was here that Uncle George pondered upon the strange ways of the world and men, and the stranger, unfathomable ways of women. (He was a bachelor and rather wary of women in general.) It was here also that he spent his time thinking of new schemes or even newer schemes when the earlier ones went awry as they sometimes did. And there are lots of schemes and adventures in this rollicking and affectionate portrait.

160pp 216mm × 135mm
ISBN 0 86299 444 6 (paper) £4.95

THE FLOWER OF GLOSTER

E. TEMPLE THURSTON

In 1911 Temple Thurston hired a canal boat, *The Flower of Gloster* and travelled the waterways of central England.

From Oxford he and his barge companion, Eynsham Harry, drifted northwards to Warwick and Stratford-on-Avon, then south-westwards to Tewkesbury and finally through the Golden Valley and Sapperton Tunnel to Lechlade.

It was probably the last time such a journey could be made, through a countryside and waterways system that had remained unchanged from the dawn of the canal age. As such, his record of their travels remains unique in its description of the rural scene and the way of life of the boat people.

176pp 248mm × 172mm
Illustrated
ISBN 0 86299 305 9 (paper) £6.95